USAF WARRIOR STUDIES

Richard H. Kohn and Joseph P. Harahan
General Editors

USAF WARRIOR STUDIES

Air Superiority in World War II and Korea, edited by Richard H. Kohn and Joseph P. Harahan, 1983
GPO Stock # 008-070-0489-5

The Command of the Air, by Guilio Douhet, 1983
GPO Stock # 008-070-0505-1

Condensed Analysis of the Ninth Air Force in the European Theater of Operations, 1984
GPO Stock # 008-070-0513-1

The Literature of Aeronautics, Astronautics, and Air Power, by Richard P. Hallion, 1984
GPO Stock # 008-070-0523-9

Over the Hump, by William H. Tunner, 1985
For distribution within the U.S. Air Force only

Air Interdiction in World War II, Korea, and Vietnam, edited by Richard H. Kohn and Joseph P. Harahan, 1986
GPO Stock # 008-070-00571-9

AIR LEADERSHIP

Proceedings of a Conference
at Bolling Air Force Base
April 13–14, 1984

Sponsored by the Air Force Historical
Foundation, the American Military Institute,
and the Military Classics Seminar

Edited with an introduction
by Wayne Thompson

Office of Air Force History
United States Air Force
Washington, D.C., 1986

Library of Congress Cataloging-in-Publication Data

Air Leadership.

    (USAF warrior studies)
    Bibliography: p. 147
    Includes index.
    1. Aeronautics, Military—United States—History—Congresses. 2. Leadership—Congresses. I. Thompson, Wayne, 1945–   . II. Air Force Historical Foundation. III. American Military Institute. IV. Military Classics Seminar. V. Series.
UG633.A6575   358.4'00973   86-18196
ISBN 0-912799-37-4

    Project Warrior Studies are published by the Office of Air Force History. The views expressed in this publication are those of the participants and do not necessarily reflect the policies of the United States Air Force or the Department of Defense.

Foreword

Air Leadership is part of a continuing series of historical volumes produced by the Office of Air Force History in direct support of Project Warrior. Since its beginnings in 1982, Project Warrior has captured the imagination of Air Force people around the world and reawakened a keener appreciation of our fundamental purpose as a Service: to deter war, but to be prepared to fight and win should deterrence fail.

Military history helps provide a realistic perspective on warfare. Through the study of past events, we gain insight into the capabilities of armed forces and, most importantly, a sound knowledge of the policies, strategies, tactics, doctrine, leadership, and weapons that have produced success in battle. Each of us, in broadening our knowledge of air power's past, halps to maintain the most effective Air Force possible, now and in the future.

LARRY D. WELCH, General, USAF
Chief of Staff

United States Air Force Historical Advisory Committee
(As of January 1, 1986)

Mr. DeWitt S. Copp
United States Information Agency

Dr. Philip A. Crowl
Annapolis, Maryland

Dr. Warren B. Hassler, Jr.
Pennsylvania State University

Brig. Gen. Harris B. Hull,
USAF, Retired
National Aeronautics and Space Administration

Dr. Alfred F. Hurley,
Brig. Gen. USAF, Retired
North Texas State University

Dr. Haskell M. Monroe, Jr.
University of Texas at El Paso

Lt. Gen. Thomas C. Richards,
USAF
Commander, Air University

Gen. Thomas M. Ryan, Jr.,
USAF, Retired

Lt. Gen. Winfield W. Scott, Jr.,
USAF
Superintendent, USAF Academy

Mr. Eugene R. Sullivan
The General Counsel, USAF

Contents

	Page
Foreword	i
Introduction	v

I. Models

Carl Spaatz: A Model for Leadership?
   David R. Mets 3
General Carl Spaatz and the Art of Command
   I. B. Holley, Jr. 15
Discussion
   Brian S. Gunderson, chair
   Mark E. Bradley, Jr.
   Alfred Goldberg
   I. B. Holley
   Curtis E. LeMay
   David R. Mets 39

II. Portraits

DeWitt Copp's Portrait of American Air Leadership
   Henry A. Probert 59
Discussion
   William S. Dudley, chair
   Henry A. Probert 73

III. Patterns

Reflections
   Alfred F. Hurley 81
Navy Air Leadership: Rear Admiral William A. Moffett as Chief of the
   Bureau of Aeronautics
   Thomas C. Hone 83

Air Force Leadership and Business Methods: Some Suggestions for Biographers
   Harry R. Borowski 119

Comment
   Allan R. Millett 131
   Bryce Poe, II 135
Discussion
   Alfred F. Hurley, chair
   Harry R. Borowski
   Thomas C. Hone
   Allan R. Millett
   Bryce Poe, II 139

Suggestions for Further Reading 147
Participants 151
Index 153

Photographs

Gen. Carl A. Spaatz 2
Gen. Ira C. Eaker 58
Rear Adm. William A. Moffett 80

Introduction

More than 200 airmen and historians met in Washington, D.C., on April 13 and 14, 1984, to discuss the men who have led American air forces. The first century of air power is drawing to a close and though some retired air leaders joined in the discussion, many have passed from the scene. What kind of men were they? What kind of leaders were they? What can we learn from their experience?

The conference approached broad questions of leadership by taking a close look at two air leaders, Rear Adm. William A. Moffett (1869–1933) and Gen. Carl A. Spaatz (1891–1974). While Chief of the Navy's Bureau of Aeronautics during the 1920s, Moffett did as much as anyone to nurture air power within the Navy. Spaatz, on the other hand, helped to lead the increasingly autonomous Army Air Forces during World War II and became the first Chief of Staff of the independent Air Force when it separated from the Army in 1947.

Despite the major roles played by Moffett and Spaatz in the development of American air power, there has been little biographical work on them until recently. A decade ago Alfred Goldberg, chief historian in the Office of the Secretary of Defense, contributed an essay on Spaatz to Field Marshal Sir Michael Carver's *The War Lords*. Richard G. Davis, an Air Force historian, has just completed a dissertation on Spaatz's service in World War II. Meanwhile the Air Force Historical Foundation has sponsored a biography of Spaatz by Lt. Col. David R. Mets, USAF, Retired, and the first fruit of his effort is one of two essays on Spaatz published here; the other is by Maj. Gen. I. B. Holley, Jr., USAFR, Retired, who has drawn upon his many years as a professor of military history and biographer.

For an assessment of Moffett, the conference turned not to a biographer but to Thomas C. Hone, a political scientist with a strong interest in the ways naval leaders dealt with new technology during the 1920s and 1930s. Moffett was one of those early air leaders who came to the new technology of air power after success in a more traditional career. He graduated from the U.S. Naval Academy at Annapolis in 1890, over a decade before the first powered airplane flight. He served under Commodore George Dewey in the Philippines during the Spanish-American War. Sixteen years later, in 1914, Moffett commanded a light cruiser when American forces seized Vera Cruz during the Mexican Revolution; his daring won him the Medal of Honor. Not until World War I and his command of the Great Lakes Naval Training Station in Illinois did Moffett begin to think much about aviation. Though he never learned to fly, he became an ardent advocate of air power.

As Chief of the Bureau of Aeronautics, Moffett was the leading figure in Navy aviation from 1921 until 1933, when he died in the crash of the dirigible *Akron*. His zest for politics and publicity served naval aviation well in its struggle to supplant the battleship with the aircraft carrier. The interdependence of aircraft carriers and aircraft helped Moffett and the Navy avoid the pressures which would eventually break the Army in two. His counterpart in the Army was Maj. Gen. Mason M. Patrick, Chief of the Air Service, who had also come to aviation late in his career. Patrick's efforts to build an air force within the Army and Moffett's comparable efforts in the Navy were often overshadowed by the calls of younger Army air officers for an independent air force which would absorb both Army and Navy aviation.

Brig. Gen. William "Billy" Mitchell led the movement for an independent air force. His court-martial in 1925 tested the loyalties of young Army air officers like Spaatz and his friend Maj. Henry "Hap" Arnold. Their testimony for Mitchell helped to secure their places in a small group of men who would mold the Air Force.

During World War II, Arnold served in Washington as Commanding General of the Army Air Forces, while Spaatz commanded the U.S. Strategic Air Forces in Europe. They were a formidable team—Arnold the impatient entrepreneur and Spaatz the patient tactician. As young graduates of the U.S. Military Academy at West Point, they had learned to fly before the United States entered World War I. Arnold was five years older, but Spaatz got the combat experience Arnold lacked—in 1918 Spaatz shot down three German fighter aircraft and was shot down himself. Spaatz's easygoing style nevertheless proved consistent with a long life, for he outlived Arnold by nearly a quarter of a century.

To probe Spaatz's role in the history of air power, this conference did not rely entirely on historians. It looked also to the Cold War generation of Air Force leaders who had served under Spaatz. No one in that generation was more influential than Gen. Curtis E. LeMay. He had become famous for his bombing tactics in both the European and Pacific theaters of World War II. He built the Strategic Air Command in the 1950s and became Air Force Chief of Staff in the early 1960s. LeMay arrived at the conference with Gen. Mark E. Bradley, Jr., who was in charge of the Air Force Logistics Command when LeMay was Chief of Staff.

While discussing Spaatz and Moffett, the conference considered the merits of biography as a tool for studying leadership. Each of the conference sessions was built around a different kind of biography. The opening session grappled not only with Spaatz but also with the possibility that he might serve as a role model for other officers. Though readers often seek a role model in biographies, biographers have reason to be wary of supplying one. It seems likely, however, that reading critical biographies can acquaint officers with leadership problems like those they may face someday. There is at least as much to learn from the mistakes of men like Spaatz and Moffett as from their successes.

Instead of providing role models, historians can produce straightforward narrative and analysis. Popular history has always depended on telling an absorbing story with vivid description. These ingredients are plentiful in DeWitt S. Copp's books on the Army Air Corps before World War II and the Army Air Forces during that war. Sponsored by the Air Force Historical Foundation, *A Few Great Captains* and *Forged in Fire* have become springboards for Foundation-sponsored biographies of Spaatz and others. Copp painted a group portrait of the officers who rallied around Mitchell in the 1920s and later led the Army Air Forces. The conference's treatment of Copp's work matched it in vividness. An evening thunderstorm punctuated the comments of Air Commodore Henry A. Probert, who has headed the Air Historical Branch in the Ministry of Defence since his retirement from active duty in the Royal Air Force. He spoke movingly of the American airmen who joined forces with British airmen against Adolf Hitler's Germany.

The next morning the conference turned its attention to scholars who are using biography to help define patterns of change. Thomas C. Hone's paper on Admiral Moffett was paired with a plea by Lt. Col. Harry R. Borowski of the Air Force Academy for more attention to the increasingly complex management problems which have confronted air leaders. Indeed Hone's paper was a good example of the kind of work needed to fill Borowski's prescription. Their thoughts about leadership and management opened a lively discussion in which the authors were joined by Col. Allan R. Millett, USMCR, of Ohio State University and Gen. Bryce Poe II, USAF, Retired.

The conference had planned that its last word would come from a famous naval airman and former Chairman of the Joint Chiefs of Staff, Adm. Thomas H. Moorer, USN, Retired. But when a sudden illness caused Moorer's absence, Brig. Gen. Alfred F. Hurley, USAF, Retired, Chancellor of North Texas State University and the closing session's chairman, asked General Poe to come out of the audience and join the panel. As a young officer, Poe had flown the Air Force's first combat jet reconnaissance sortie at the outset of the Korean War. Later he helped deploy the first intercontinental ballistic missiles, commanded a reconnaissance wing in Vietnam, and led the Air Force Logistics Command during the late 1970s. Poe's career had involved him deeply in leadership and management questions, about which he spoke with conviction.

This conference was sponsored by the the Air Force Historical Foundation (Brig. Gen. Brian S. Gunderson, USAF, Retired, President), the American Military Institute (Edward M. Coffman, President), and the Military Classics Seminar of Washington, D.C. (William S. Dudley, Chairman). Richard H. Kohn, Lt. Col. Elliott V. Converse, and the editor coordinated conference arrangements with assistance from associates in the Office of Air Force History and elsewhere on Bolling Air Force Base. Lt. Gen. Howard W. Leaf (Assistant Vice Chief of Staff, U.S. Air Force) and Col. Edward R. Maney (Commander, 1100th Air Base Wing) generously supported the conference and participated in it. Hugh N. Ahmann of the U.S. Air Force Historical Research Center's Oral History Division tape-recorded the sessions; Beth Scott of the Division transcribed them. Vanessa D. Allen of the Office of Air Force History prepared the manuscript for publication.

Wayne Thompson
Office of Air Force History

I. MODELS

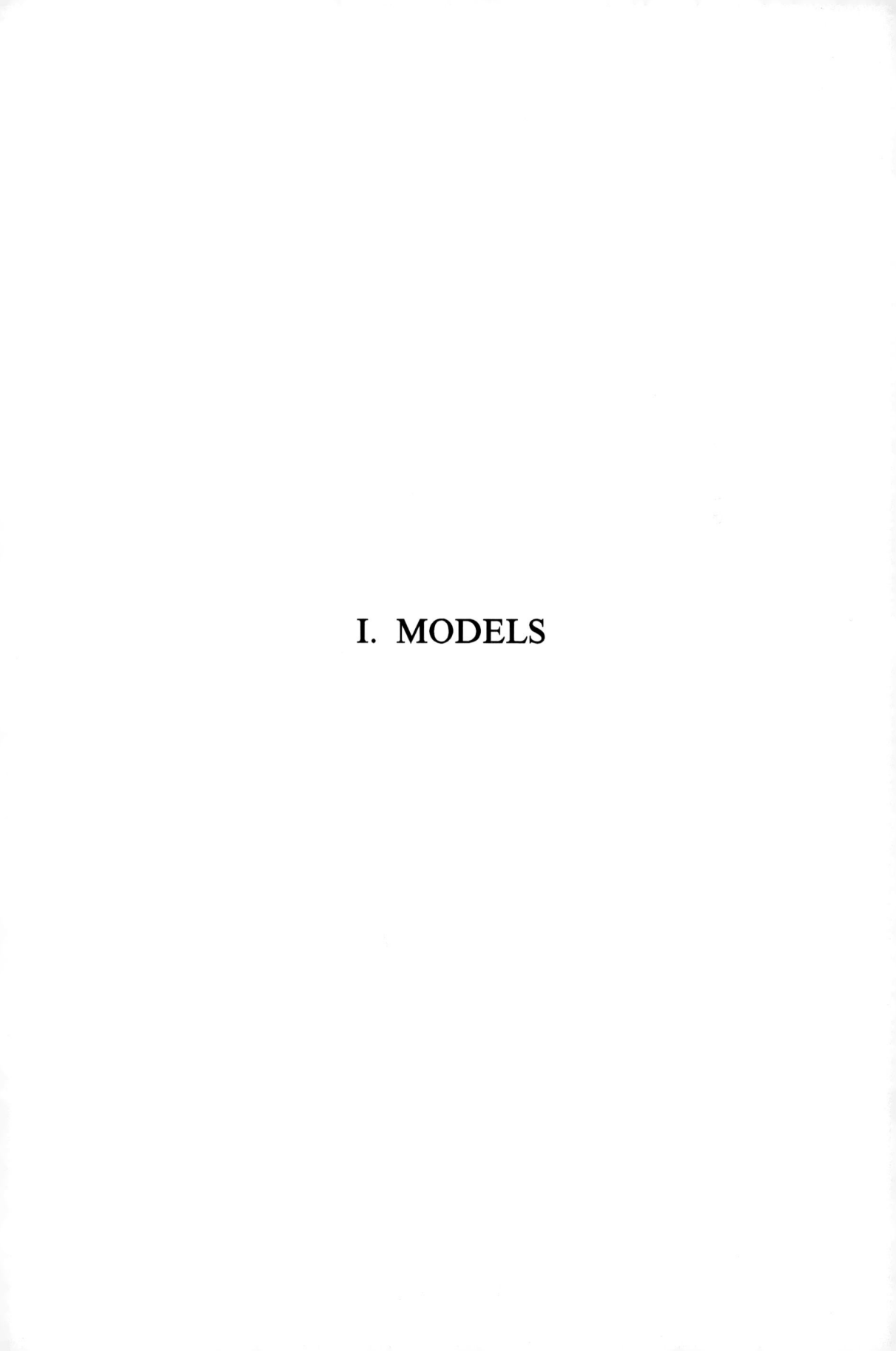

Gen. Carl A. Spaatz
1891–1974

Carl Spaatz was so unusual a leader that his record challenges anyone who would try to squeeze successful leadership into a single mold. Spaatz's biographer, Lt. Col. David Mets, USAF, Retired, admires Spaatz's calm delegation of authority in North Africa and Europe during World War II. But Maj. Gen. I.B. Holley, Jr., USAFR, Retired, of Duke University finds that Spaatz earlier made a major error when in 1940 he vetoed the development of drop tanks necessary to give fighter aircraft enough fuel for escorting bombers on long missions. Apparently Spaatz was less effective as a staff division chief in Washington than he would be later as a commander of air forces at war. Since different situations call for different kinds of leadership, officers who seek a role model may find that they need more than one.—W.T.

Carl Spaatz: A Model for Leadership?

David R. Mets

Speculation on the nature of leadership may be almost as old as humanity. Yet it appears we are hardly any closer to a consensus than we have ever been. There is not even agreement on whether leadership is a science, an art, or some combination of the two. Successful military leaders who claim that leadership is indeed an art—that it is important to be one's self above all else—nevertheless go on to list leadership traits and methods as if these could be learned. Nearly two centuries after the founding of the U.S. Military Academy at West Point, some are still uncertain about which process is more important: the teaching of leadership or the "selection out" of cadets who lack a full measure of the traits thought desirable.[1] Whatever our preference on that issue, we have made a tremendous investment in academies and war colleges. But can we construct a model of the ideal leader toward which those institutions should work?

Historians may flinch at the sound of the word "model." Courses in historiography usually emphasize that history does *not* repeat itself—that the purpose of reading history (beyond mere entertainment) is primarily to broaden one's perspective. The number of variables in history is so immense that the odds are very much against them combining in exactly the same way on any two occasions. Consequently, the lessons of history must always be what *can*, not what *will* happen. If a model is to serve as a teaching aid or a vehicle for communication, we may use it. But if it is to provide concrete laws or a catechism for lieutenants, most historians would object that too much is asked.

A model is an abstraction of reality, a simplification of the real world, an ideal form. A man need not reach the ideal to be a successful leader. He may even flagrantly violate the ideal and still achieve success. Practically every prescription for leadership I have seen at military schools has demanded integrity above all else. Yet Napoleon lied with abandon, had people murdered, and cheated his own mother at cards.[2] Any model for leadership, then, must be heavily qualified.

When military commanders define leadership models in terms of personal traits, integrity is almost always there; as is courage, both physical and moral.[3] Fairness in dealing with troops and concern for their welfare are

AIR LEADERSHIP

usually in the model. One would suppose that broad professional knowledge is universally deemed to be essential, and it is nearly so.[4] The ability to communicate with both subordinates and bosses seems to be valued. Good physical conditioning is often stressed.[5] Perhaps patriotism and personal appearance are rarely mentioned because they are so obvious. Beyond such generalities, there is not much agreement. Some would have a leader inflexibly set an example for followers; others think that flexibility on nonessentials conserves strength for stands on fundamental issues. Often admired, but one suspects less often practiced, is the openness of mind which permits a leader to listen to followers and change his views.[6]

Gen. Carl Spaatz did much to equip America with air power. He commanded the U.S. Strategic Air Forces in Europe during the Second World War, and later he was the first Chief of Staff of the independent Air Force. Yet his life story could provide a young lieutenant with a prescription for disaster—a virtual guarantee that he would never get near enough to the levers of power to lead much of anything.

Within three weeks of Spaatz's arrival at West Point in 1910, he tried to select himself out by resigning.[7] He was prevailed upon to change his mind on that occasion, but was later nearly expelled for the possession of liquor. It was said that he avoided expulsion only through a technicality—a procedure hardly to be recommended to cadets of the 1980s.[8] Still less to be recommended was a half-hearted effort in academics (number 57 out of 107) and a truly poor conduct record (number 95). He was still walking punishment tours on graduation day, when his nickname "Tooey" must have seemed especially appropriate; thanks to his red hair and freckles, Spaatz resembled Francis J. Toohey, who graduated last in the previous class.[9]

Spaatz is now remembered mostly as a bomber commander, but during the First World War he shot down three Fokkers over the Western Front. In those dogfights, he sometimes forgot one of the cardinal rules of being either a model pilot or a great military leader: one must always "check six" (that is, look for enemy aircraft on his tail) if he is to survive long enough to become a leader at all. Major Spaatz was hard on the tail of one Fokker, when another closed on Spaatz's tail.[10] Even after his squadron commander, Capt. Charles J. Biddle, zoomed down to shoot the German off Spaatz's tail, Spaatz violated yet another canon of living long enough to lead: he did not disengage in time to make it back to friendly lines. Out of fuel, he crashed in "No Man's Land." Fortunately, the first voices he heard from the trenches were French.[11] This incident illustrates not a model to be consciously followed, but a leadership trait thought by Napoleon to be among the most desirable: luck.

In 1924 when Spaatz came away from his command of the First Pursuit Group at Selfridge Field, Michigan, his record carried a reprimand from the Adjutant General of the Army that cited "dense ignorance of . . . duties."[12] Spaatz had tried to help a finance officer whose drinking and gambling led eventually to embezzling. It was not to be the last black mark on Spaatz's record. When he left the Command and General Staff College at Fort Leavenworth in 1935, an annotation explicitly recommended against Spaatz's assignment to high command and staff duties.[13]

There was much in Spaatz's early record that could serve better as a caution than as a guide, but he absorbed a practical education that would serve him well. During the First World War (when he was less than four years out of West Point), Spaatz took command of America's largest flying training center at Issoudun, France. Arriving just as the buildup was beginning, he encountered almost every problem imaginable in training and most of the logistical problems found anywhere in the Air Service. After the war, whenever he was not commanding a pursuit or bomber unit, he was posted to Washington. There he studied all manner of organizational, technical, strategic, and tactical subjects. He was tutored by William "Billy" Mitchell and exchanged ideas with Henry "Hap" Arnold and Ira C. Eaker.

Spaatz sat on many procurement boards which hammered out specifications for new airplanes. He testified before committees trying to fit those planes into America's national security structure. He engaged in a continuing correspondence with instructors at the Air Corps Tactical School and engineers at the Materiel Division who sought his advice. In 1938 when Oscar Westover was killed in an aircraft accident and Arnold replaced him as Chief of the Air Corps, he made Spaatz head of his plans division. Two years later Arnold sent Spaatz to observe the Battle of Britain.

The breadth of Spaatz's experience, however, does not emerge fully from a list of his assignments. Indeed his early career might now seem too narrow, too confined to operations. Today's Air Force encourages varied assignments with logistical and technical commands or even other services. But the Air Corps of the interwar period was much smaller than the Air Force of today. It had fewer than two thousand officers when the buildup for World War II began in 1938. Consequently, Spaatz knew a large portion of them and knew much about their work.

In any case, Spaatz was relaxed about his career prospects. One example of his deep inner security comes from his home life in the 1920s. An Army wife was expected to be a homemaker and to stay away from conspicuous, commercial enterprises such as the professional theater. Yet while Spaatz was assigned to the Washington staff of Maj. Gen. Mason Patrick, Chief of the Air Service, Ruth Spaatz was commuting to Baltimore where she appeared

AIR LEADERSHIP

on the professional stage. To this day she maintains that her husband never showed an iota of resentment, or even concern, but seemed rather proud of her.[14]

There was a playful side to Spaatz that contributed to his fitness for leadership. Medium of stature, trim of figure, and quick on his feet, he gained renown as a builder of squash courts and organizer of squash tournaments during the twenties and thirties.[15] In later years though he ceased to have an active exercise program, he never gained much more than ten pounds. A gregarious person throughout his long life, he would not give up drinking and smoking (despite at least one strong lecture from a flight surgeon about the latter habit).[16]

Though not especially ambitious for himself, Spaatz did want a separate air force which would not be controlled by the Army or the Navy. He had become close to Billy Mitchell—almost a protege. Their relationship began in France during the First World War and matured during Spaatz's tenure as commander at Selfridge Field in the early twenties. Since Mitchell was then courting his second wife who lived in nearby Detroit, he found frequent excuses to inspect Spaatz's unit, the only Army pursuit group. As Mitchell's service came to its dramatic end, Spaatz won a reputation for moral courage at the famous trial in 1925; he blurted out strong words in support of Mitchell while the court was trying to repress further comments.[17]

When Spaatz became commander of the U.S. Strategic Air Forces in Europe during World War II, his consuming goal was victory over Hitler. To that end, Spaatz sought cooperative relations with ground commanders. Even Hap Arnold, the Commanding General of the Army Air Forces, did not push for creation of a separate air force during the war. Only after the war did Arnold and Spaatz lead a successful drive for an independent air force.

If one classifies leadership styles into "authoritarian" or "charismatic," then Spaatz must be put into the latter category—though his was a quiet charisma. If the divisions are "methodical" or "pragmatic," then he again belongs in the latter. If "mercurial" or "steady," then the choice is certainly "steady."

One way to understand Spaatz better is to examine his relationships with two of his famous contemporaries, Dwight D. Eisenhower and George S. Patton. Patton was one of Spaatz's favorite ground generals, though Patton's leadership style was quite different. Patton was aggressive, and Spaatz liked that; he too was aggressive, especially as a tactician. But Spaatz was not much given to posturing in public. Aside from taking the grommet out of his garrison cap (an old Air Corps custom dating from the twenties), he kept his uniform neat and conventional—no polished helmets or pearl-handled revolvers for him. Patton read more deeply in military history, though Spaatz did prefer history to fiction.[18] Perhaps Patton had a more ambitious intellect, or perhaps Spaatz had an airman's tendency to discount the importance of events before the Wright brothers.

Eisenhower and Spaatz worked together through most of World War II and the postwar unification struggle. They had known each other since West Point, where Eisenhower was in the class after Spaatz. Though not showmen, neither Eisenhower nor Spaatz was blind to the importance of public relations. Far from it. Both were adept at handling the press—much more so than Patton—and Spaatz built some enduring friendships among newsmen.[19]

Spaatz and Eisenhower were compatible, but their views were far from identical. Notwithstanding his engaging personality, Eisenhower had a sterner outlook on life. He once wondered if Spaatz was tough enough for high command and if he were too much given to cronyism. During the North African campaign, Spaatz and his staff were housed in an elegant villa overlooking the sea. Later, when the Army Air Forces set up a rest and recreational facility at Capri, one of Spaatz's subordinates reserved the most elegant villa there for Eisenhower and the second most opulent for Spaatz. When Eisenhower found out about it, he opened the villas to all officers.[20] On the other hand, Spaatz had a very wide reputation for informality. Judging from Eisenhower's letters to his wife, one is tempted to say that he did show a bit more concern with his own rank than did Spaatz.

Spaatz appeared to enjoy life more than Eisenhower did. Even while the Battle of the Bulge was raging in December 1944, Spaatz found time for card games.[21] His game was poker; Eisenhower's was bridge. Spaatz relished his game far into the night with a bottle of scotch at hand; Eisenhower liked to retire early with a western novel. Eisenhower drove himself to the point where on more than one occasion, the Army Chief of Staff, General George Marshall, ordered him to take a rest. Spaatz seemed relatively relaxed and did not make a point of arriving at the office early.

But Spaatz had a way of incorporating work into play. His poker games were staff meetings. His big quarters permitted key staff members and visiting subordinates to live with him. The American air force was a daylight bombing organization, which meant that the men who led it inevitably became night owls. Decisions for the next day's operations could not be made until the current day's results were available, usually in the evening. Moreover, the weather in Europe was so changeable that it forced commanders to delay their target choices until the last minute. So in an informal way, the work of Spaatz's headquarters proceeded around the clock.[22]

AIR LEADERSHIP

In the spring of 1944, Eisenhower decided to divert heavy bombers from German targets to French railyards in preparation for sending allied soldiers across the English Channel. Spaatz told Eisenhower in no uncertain terms that diversion of the bombers was wrong: if not permitted to apply some air power against oil targets in Germany, Spaatz could no longer see his way clear to command U.S. Strategic Air Forces in Europe.[23] Since there could then have been little doubt that the allies would ultimately win the war, a skeptic might be inclined to see Spaatz's stand as an attempt to increase the glory of the air arm in hope of winning independence after the war. Yet it was also already clear that Eisenhower might be influential in the postwar world and his support for a separate air force might be essential to success. Eisenhower was famous for his insistence on harmony among allies and was hard on Americans who violated it; Spaatz's opposition largely took the form of trying to keep control of his strategic air forces away from Air Chief Marshal Sir Trafford Leigh-Mallory, the British commander of allied tactical air forces supporting the cross-channel attack. We may be justified, then, in seeing a measure of both honesty and moral courage in Spaatz's stand.

Though Spaatz could take a stand, he was neither a dogmatic supporter of his own ideas nor a reckless hard-charger ready to waste other men's lives. When in the fall of 1944 Air Chief Marshal Sir Arthur Tedder, Eisenhower's British deputy, again advocated a railyard campaign, Spaatz permitted himself to be persuaded.[24] By then his favorite targets, the German oil plants, were pretty well beaten up and through ULTRA intelligence he knew it. Another reason he had disparaged the earlier railyard plan was that he believed the Luftwaffe would not come up to defend the yards and be destroyed before being brought to bear against the Normandy landings. Now Normandy was behind him. His force had grown large enough so that he could devote part of it, even the greater part, to Tedder's targets and still have enough to keep the pressure on the German liquid fuel plants.[25]

Carl Spaatz ever preferred to lead by giving a subordinate a job and leaving the details of the work to him—Spaatz held the reins with a loose hand. Some, like Eisenhower, would say that a corollary should have been readiness to relieve a subordinate who did not measure up. There is little evidence in Spaatz's papers to show that he was much inclined to fire a man. Since the Air Corps had been such a tiny fraction of the Army during the interwar period, Spaatz knew nearly everybody with substantial experience in the air; that may have looked more like cronyism than it actually was. Then too, there were just not enough failures among his subordinate commanders to have thoroughly tested him on the point.

In early 1944 when he thought that Eighth Air Force was not determined enough to persist in bad weather missions, Spaatz did threaten to relieve the commander, Maj. Gen. James H. Doolittle. But this threat was never carried out, perhaps thanks to a shared experience. They were airborne together when the weather closed every airfield in England and forced their pilot to land in a pasture. In any case, the weather problem lessened with the coming of spring, the installation of electronic landing aids, and the development of radar bombing.[26]

Every commander must be a kind of junction box between the men below who pay the personal price to get the job done and the men above who want to see results. Spaatz's pragmatism helped him with both sets of relations. The 1943 losses suffered by Eighth Air Force had meant that the odds against a crew member completing a twenty-five-mission tour were worse than four to one. When Spaatz moved from the Mediterranean to England at the end of 1943, he informed Arnold that bombers would not be sent beyond escort range except in unusual circumstances and that escort range would be extended as quickly as possible.[27] Since there was solid evidence that experienced crews were much less vulnerable than new ones, he attempted a new policy of sending crews home for a thirty-day leave to revive their morale for a return to combat. Arnold's chief of staff, Lt. Gen. Barney Giles, soon reported that the morale of men coming back to the embarkation points was still too low.[28] Spaatz was pragmatic enough to drop the program and go back to a fixed-length tour that gave flyers hope.

Spaatz's concern for his men was evident again and again. During the summer of 1944, Spaatz resisted the assignment of his heavy bombers to attacks on V–1 cruise missile launching sites. Though he was ready to accept casualties when they helped to shorten the war, V–1 sites were antiaircraft traps that would lure bombers away from the German heartland.[29] Because Churchill and Eisenhower insisted on using bombers against the V–1, Spaatz did not get his way.[30] Meanwhile, when Arnold questioned the motivations of crews landing their bombers in Sweden after receiving battle damage over German targets, Spaatz cabled back immediately that the charges were "slander" and totally false. He demanded and got an investigation which found the internees free of cowardice.[31]

Spaatz had a good understanding of the problems troubling those above him too. The relationship between Arnold and Spaatz dated back to the time of the First World War and was unshakeable. Spaatz could stand up to the boss, but Spaatz understood obstacles in Washington as well as Arnold's need to prepare the way for a solution of postwar difficulties. Arnold wanted to compile an air record during the war that would earn respect; at the same time, he wanted to cultivate the friendship of those who would have an important voice after the peace finally came. Spaatz's relationship with Eisenhower was important in this regard, and Spaatz also took care whenever

AIR LEADERSHIP

he had to deal directly with the Army Chief of Staff, General Marshall. In March 1945, for example, Marshall sent Spaatz to neutral Switzerland after navigational mistakes caused some of Spaatz's planes to attack Basel and Zurich. Spaatz apologized to the Swiss and explained to Marshall that technological progress would soon greatly enhance the potential of strategic bombing. Marshall was already pretty well sold on the idea of a separate air force.[32] After the war, both he and Eisenhower would support air independence.

It is difficult to judge the impact of leadership, because such a judgment entails an estimate of what did not happen as well as what did. Seldom in military history has a campaign of the winning side had a more thorough critique than did that of Spaatz's U.S. Strategic Air Forces in Europe. At the initiative of the Air Staff, President Roosevelt commissioned a group under the leadership of insurance executive Franklin D'Olier to investigate the conduct and the effects of the strategic bombing campaign.

That group, known as the U.S. Strategic Bombing Survey, did not satisfy some of the most avid air enthusiasts, for it concluded that air power had been *a* (not *the*) decisive factor in winning the war. Their report did suggest that a modern industrial state could not long exist when it lost air superiority over its heartland. Even though Spaatz was later to speak with reservation of the survey, it gave his work at least a partial vote of confidence. The flaw was that air power took longer than he had hoped, and the armies crossed the borders of the Reich simultaneously with the climax of the strategic bombing effort. In Japan conventional bombing was overshadowed by two atomic bombs. So conventional air power's effects were less apparent to others than to airmen.[33]

The Allies almost certainly would have won the Second World War without Spaatz. There would have been a massive strategic bombardment campaign anyway, but as Alfred Goldberg and others have suggested, the emphasis on oil targets might not have been as heavy or as early.[34] According to the Strategic Bombing Survey, the oil attack had a major impact on the functioning of the Nazi war machine.[35] The war might well have been longer, and more Allied soldiers might have died, were it not for Spaatz.

The air arm came out of the war with a prestige that was an important asset in the campaign for Spaatz's other great goal, the establishment of an autonomous air force. In 1947 the Air Force got its independence, but not control over Navy and Marine Corps aviation. The attempt to unify the services in a Department of Defense was also restrained by the Navy, so that the new Secretary of Defense was for several years merely a coordinator of service policies. Spaatz played a role in these compromises, since he was taken to be less of a firebrand than other Army Air Forces officers.[36] According to Adm. Arthur Radford, Spaatz even offered to help him become chief of staff of a separate and unified air arm.[37]

It is hard to say what would have happened if Spaatz's attitude had been more uncompromising—the outcome might have been either worse or better. But as Spaatz explained to an apparently disappointed Arnold, the 1947 compromise may have been the best that could have been had at the time:

> With reference to the unification compromise, I suppose there will always be a controversy over who-got-what out of the agreement. The fact that each interested party feels that the other got the best break is probably the strongest argument in favor of the soundness of the agreed scheme. So far as the Air Force is concerned, we will, under the proposed arrangement, achieve the position of independence and parity with the other services. I feel that the aircraft, air facilities and air functions not under the Air Force are at least under a top authority who can insure that they are not misapplied or used to establish a basis of encroachment on the proper activities of the Air Force. We believe that the agreement when implemented by legislation, will be a forward step for the Air Force and will represent marked progress in the operating efficiency and economy of our Armed Forces.[38]

The best that Spaatz could say for the compromise was that its implementation would be a "forward step"—no sense of triumph here. Doolittle's criticism of Billy Mitchell may help to explain Spaatz's strength. Doolittle has said that Mitchell was like a great oak tree when he should have been like bamboo.[39] Oak may snap in the hurricane, but bamboo bends and springs back when the storm is over. Spaatz was more like bamboo.

Many of Spaatz's qualities seem those least likely to be produced by deliberate cultivation. Spaatz's courage, for example, was admired. Yet for anyone to learn that quality from Spaatz or from a book (or from contact sports and survival school) does not seem very likely. Spaatz's pragmatic flexibility, however, could inspire emulation. Junior officers might also want to imitate his preference for persuasion over coercion in directing the work of subordinates. He was very much a leader who would assign a job to a subordinate and then leave him alone to accomplish it. In 1944 and 1945, Spaatz gave his subordinate commanders room to make many operational decisions, and his faith in those men proved well founded. Spaatz's leadership provides a model that can give junior officers (and senior ones as well) a helpful perspective, if not an explicit guide to action.

Notes

1. Robert Priest, *et al*, "Personality and Value Changes in West Point Cadets," *Armed Forces and Society*, 8 (Summer 1982), 629–42.
2. H.A.L. Fisher, *Napoleon*, (New York, 1912, 1950), pp 5, 76, 193 and 158; George Gordon Andrews, *Napoleon in Review*, (New York, 1939), pp 43–50, 218–19.
3. Gen Matthew B. Ridgway, USA, Ret., "Leadership," *Military Review*, XLVI (Oct 1966), 40–9; Gen Edward C. Meyer, USA, "Leadership: A Return to Basics," *Military Review*, LX (Jul 1980), 4–9; Lt Gen Jack C. Catton, USAF, "A Personal Concept of Command," *Supplement to Air Force Policy Letter for Commanders*, Mar 1969, pp 18–25; Maj Joseph Angsten, Jr., USA, "The Battalion Commander: Linkpin in Battlefield Success," *Military Review*, LXII (Mar 1982), 84–92; Lt Col Timothy E. Cline, USAF, "Where Have All the Mitchells Gone?" *Air University Review*, XXXIII (May–Jun 1982), 23–32.
4. A startling exception is a prize-winner in the Ira C. Eaker Essay contest that offers a model that leaves out both professional knowledge and physical courage: Col Edward J. Murphy, USAF, "A Judge Advocate Shares his Views on Leadership," *Air University Review*, XXIV (Mar–Apr 1983), 23–32.
5. Ridgway, "Leadership," p 46.
6. Catton, "Personal Concept of Command," pp 20, 23.
7. US Military Academy, "Headquarters Correspondence, So-Tho," Document #8397-28, Summaries, USMA Archives, West Point, NY.
8. Maj Gen Robert Walsh, USAF, Ret., interview with David R. Mets, 31 Mar 1982, Washington, DC.
9. Mrs. Carl A. Spaatz, interview with David R. Mets, 25 Mar 1982, Washington, DC; US Military Academy, "Class Graduation Standing Cards, Form D, 1904–1914," USMA Archives, West Point, NY. There were 107 graduates in Spaatz's class; 26 of them became generals; of the 26, 12 came from the top half of the class and 14 from the bottom—Spaatz was among the latter. Clearly a high class standing need not be an element of our model. Data from Michael J. Krisman, ed., *Register of Graduates*, (West Point, NY: Associate of Graduates, USMA, 1982), pp 312–14.
10. Charles J. Biddle, *Way of the Eagle*, (New York, 1919), pp 193–95.
11. Gen Carl A. Spaatz, USAF, Ret., interview, 27 Sep 1968, USAF Academy, CO, USAF Oral History #583; and interview, 19 May 1965, USAF Oral History #755, both at USAF Historical Center, Maxwell AFB, AL.
12. Maj Gen Harry G. Hale, USA, to Adjutant General, Washington, DC, with attachments, 22 Nov 1924, in Spaatz 201 File, National Records Center, St. Louis, MO.
13. "Efficiency Report," War Department Form 67, 1 Jul 1936, in Spaatz 201 File, National Records Center, St. Louis, MO.
14. Mrs. Ruth Spaatz, interview, 3 Mar 1981, Washington, DC, USAF Oral History #1266, at USAF Historical Research Center, Maxwell AFB, AL.
15. Eaker, interview, 26 Mar 1982; Mrs. Walter Bell (Spaatz's oldest daughter Katharine), interview, 7 Mar 1983.
16. Dr. Charles Kossman, MD, in New York to Col M. Samuel White in Washington, 18 Feb 1947, #168.7082-231, USAF Historical Research Center, Maxwell AFB, AL.
17. "Mitchell Adds to Air Service Charges; Sees Perjury Plot in Shenandoah Case; Three Officers Back Him Before Court," *New York Times*, 10 Nov 1925, sec 1, p 1; Lt Gen Ira C. Eaker, interview with David R. Mets, 26 Mar 1982, Washington, DC.
18. Mrs. Walter Bell, interview with David R. Mets, 7 Mar 1983, London, UK.

AIR LEADERSHIP

19. Kenneth Crawford, interview with David R. Mets, 30 Mar 1982, Washington, DC; Steven Leo, interview with David R. Mets, Harpeswell, ME, 11 Aug 1982.
20. Dwight D. Eisenhower to Mark Wayne Clark, 27 Dec 1943, in Alfred D. Chandler, Jr., ed., *The Papers of Dwight David Eisenhower: The War Years*, Vol III (Baltimore, MD, 1970), p 1624.
21. Solly Zuckerman, *From Apes to Warlords*, (New York, 1978), p 315.
22. Gen Laurence S. Kuter, USAF, Ret., interview with Hugh Ahmann, 30 Sep–3 Oct 1975, Naples, FL, USAF Oral History #810, USAF Historical Research Center, Maxwell AFB, AL.
23. W.W. Rostow, *Pre-Invasion Bombing Strategy: General Eisenhower's Decision of March 25, 1944*, (Austin, TX, 1981), p 148.
24. Lord [Arthur] Tedder, Marshal of the Royal Air Force, *With Prejudice*, (Boston, 1966), pp 604–12.
25. Spaatz in France to Doolittle in England, 13 Dec 1944, in Spaatz Papers, Box 16.
26. Lt Gen James H. Doolittle, interview with David R. Mets, 19 May 1982, Washington, DC.
27. Msg, Spaatz in England to Arnold in Washington, 21 Jan 1944, in Spaatz Papers, Box 14.
28. Lt Gen Barney Giles in Washington to Spaatz in England, 28 May 1944, in Spaatz Papers, Box 15.
29. David Irving, *The Rise and Fall of the Luftwaffe: The Life of Field Marshal Erhard Milch*, (Boston, 1973), p 231.
30. Spaatz to Eisenhower, 28 Jun 1944, Pre-Presidential File, Box 115, Eisenhower Library, Abilene, KS; Memorandum, Eisenhower to Air Marshal Sir Arthur Tedder, 29 Jun 1944, Pre-Presidential File, Box 115, Eisenhower Library.
31. Wesley Frank Craven and James Lea Cate, eds., *The Army Air Forces in World War II*, Vol III, *Europe: Argument to V-E Day*, (Chicago, 1951), p 307.
32. Spaatz to Marshall, 13 Mar 1945; Marshall to Spaatz, 7 Mar 1945; Giles to Spaatz, 8 Mar 1945; Spaatz to Giles, 19 Mar 1945; and Arnold to Spaatz 28 Mar 1945, all in Spaatz Papers, Box 21.
33. *Overall Report (European War), US Strategic Bombing Survey*, Franklin D'Olier, chairman, 30 Sep 1945, p 107.
34. Alfred Goldberg, "Spaatz," in Field Marshal Sir Michael Carver, ed., *The Warlords: Military Commanders of the Twentieth Century*, (Boston, 1976), p 574; Rostow, *Pre-Invasion Bombing Strategy*, p 84.
35. *US Strategic Bombing Survey, Overall Report*, p 39; B.H. Liddell Hart, *The German Generals Talk*, (New York, 1948), pp 272–93.
36. Adm Arleigh Burke, USN, Ret., interview with David R. Mets, 25 Mar 83, Fort Myer VA; RAdm Thomas Davies, USN, Ret., interview with Mets, 12 Sep 83, Arlington VA. In an interview in 1965, Spaatz himself said that his single greatest contribution had been fighting for a separate Air Force—interview, 19 May 1965, USAF Oral History #755, USAF Historical Research Center, Maxwell AFB, AL.
37. Stephen Jurika, ed., *From Pearl Harbor to Vietnam: The Memoirs of Admiral Arthur W. Radford* (Stanford, CA, 1980), p 82.
38. Spaatz in Washington to Arnold in California, 5 Feb 1947, in Spaatz Papers, Box 256.
39. Doolittle, interview 19 May 1982, and interview 26 Sep 1971, USAF Oral History #793, USAF Historical Research Center, Maxwell AFB, AL.

General Carl Spaatz and the Art of Command*

I. B. Holley, Jr.

Officers who aspire to flag rank have a powerful incentive to study a wide variety of styles and modes of command. All who engage in this indoor sport doubtlessly hope that it will be career-enhancing and carry them to the top, but the realities of promotion are decidedly uneven. Some who richly deserve it do indeed reach flag rank. A few who do not deserve it may also acquire stars—by virtue of political pull, accidents of time or place, and the like. Some who richly deserve it will not reach flag rank. There are more able men who attain the rank of colonel than there are slots for stars, and much depends on timing, the luck of the draw, who happens to sit on a promotion board, and other similar variables.

What makes one officer's leadership better than another's? Every student of military leadership can readily compile a long list of qualities he deems essential to success. Many of these qualities turn out to be overlapping or comparable terms merely expressed in different ways. As the art critic Bernard Berenson once said, "All representation involves a compromise with chaos." To reduce the number of ideas about leadership to manageable proportions, those ideas can be gathered under three headings, three symbolic terms: guts, imagination, and objectivity. After using these terms to fashion a yardstick, we can try it out on the Air Force's first Chief of Staff, Gen. Carl Spaatz.

The term "guts" embraces both physical courage and moral courage, another term for character—the prime requisite of all truly great leaders. It takes moral courage to relieve a subordinate from an important command in the heat of battle because he has failed to perform, even though he has been your best friend for years—as Gen. John J. Pershing relieved his own Academy roommate in France during World War I. It takes moral courage to command an aircraft carrier in battle and resolutely refuse to break radio silence and endanger the whole operation, even when you can hear that lost

---

*Ed. note: This paper, which was not presented at the conference, develops ideas advanced by Professor Holley in "Of Saber Charges, Escort Fighters, and Spacecraft," *Air University Review* XXIV, 6 (Sep–Oct 1983), 2–11.

AIR LEADERSHIP

fighter pilot out there in the night pleading for a homing signal because he is running out of fuel—and you know that pilot is your dearest friend's son.

Loyalty also takes guts, because it involves both telling your chief what he does not want to hear and backing your subordinate even when his mistakes get you into trouble. The diaries of Count Galeazzo Ciano, Benito Mussolini's son-in-law, contain a revealing account of the dictator's relationship with his army chief of staff, Marshal Pietro Badoglio.[1] In the fall of 1940, Badoglio thought that Italy was not adequately prepared to attack Greek forces in Albania. But he was afraid to confront Mussolini, who was in a mood to accept Badoglio's resignation. Only after the Italian offensive stalled did Badoglio resign. Though he was then a convenient scapegoat for Mussolini, Badoglio eventually helped to oust his former boss. Lacking mutual loyalty, their relationship was built on weakness rather than courage.

Another manifestation of guts is the desire to seek responsibility and the willingness to accept responsibility when it is thrust upon one. It is one thing to be given command of a well-armed, well-trained, high-spirited force eager to prove itself against a hated enemy, but it is quite another matter to assume command of a badly battered force dispirited from a long retreat. Ask yourself how enthusiastic you would have been if in 1917 the King of Italy had ordered you to take command of the Italian army as it fell back from the disaster at Caporetto? Guts are the necessary ingredient of that determination to see it through when one is seemingly overwhelmed by exhaustion, discouragement, frustration, and defeatism. Perhaps the final word on guts is Winston Churchill's observation that courage is the "quality which guarantees all others."[2]

The second essential quality for command is imagination. That word conjures up many notions, but above all it connotes vision. Imagination suggests an ability to conceptualize, to reach ahead in the mind and to anticipate, to construct a picture of what might be, to envision. Imagination involves receptivity, an openness to novel ideas. For a positive example of this kind of leadership, one has only to recall the receptivity of Churchill to such daring ideas as the tank in World War I or the floating artificial harbors in World War II.

For a fine rendering of a defective imagination, one should read C. S. Forester's satirical novel *The General* with its depiction of an opaque military mind. This unflattering picture, we are told, was translated into German just before World War II and read widely in Nazi military circles, a circumstance which may help explain why the Germans sometimes underestimated their British opponents.[3]

An imaginative leader is creative; he is able to concoct a clear conception of objectives; and he can visualize alternative courses of action—which is to say, his imagination is disciplined to the point where he has perfected the knack of setting the ends desired against the means available.

As an illustration of creative imagination at work in a gifted leader of men, consider the example of Col. T. E. Lawrence, the Englishman who played such a dramatic role in freeing the Arabs from Turkish domination. He understood how inadequate were the means at his disposal, a cluster of Arab tribesmen fiercely independent, ill-equipped, and as much at loggerheads with one another as with the enemy. Any attempt to get them together for a frontal assault on the Turks was almost certain to fail. So Lawrence took the measure of the limited means at his disposal and devised an imaginative strategy which was within the capabilities of his forces. His fast-moving, camel-mounted Bedouin guerrillas would appear suddenly and unexpectedly at unlikely spots and blow up railroad bridges on either side of a Turkish troop train moving through the desert; they would destroy and plunder, then fade away into the desert. Avoiding pitched battle insofar as possible, they wore down Turkish resistance, not only physically but psychologically. Lawrence's genius for leadership was largely a matter of imagination, not numbers or weapons.

Some men may be endowed with creative genius at birth; the rest have to get there by sustained effort. As the great French mathematician Jules Poincaré put it, "Genius strikes most often in the prepared mind."

After guts and imagination, the third essential attribute of military leadership is objectivity. To be objective one must cultivate the habit of intellectual self-reliance, thinking a problem through for oneself. But there is more to it than that; objectivity requires the cultivation of a judicious temperament, a healthy skepticism toward all proposals and propositions, especially those most ardently advocated by special pleaders with an interest at stake. Objectivity requires a disciplined mind, a mind trained first in the art of acquiring evidence and then in techniques for assessing that evidence.

A truly disciplined mind is not only trained to assess complex variables objectively, but is also habituated to this practice. The commander with a trained mind avoids leaping to conclusions; he tries to keep his personal predilections from skewing the balance. In the words of Scotland's favorite poet, Robert Burns:

> If self the wavering balance shake,
> It's rarely right adjusted.

Objectivity is not solely a matter of overcoming prejudice—the tendency to prejudge an issue; it also involves getting all the facts or at least all that it is possible to assemble. The biographer of Air Chief Marshal Lord Dowding, who led the Royal Air Force's Fighter Command during the Battle of Britain in the grim days of 1940, offers us an instructive insight on just this point.

AIR LEADERSHIP

The more senior an officer is, the more he must rely upon reports submitted by subordinates. One of the great dilemmas of the decisionmaker is how far to trust the judgment of the staff expert who is recommending some course of action with vital implications for the future. Just such an instance arose in the 1930s when Dowding headed the research staff at RAF headquarters. The question at issue was whether to build biplane or monoplane fighters. The experts advocated continuing with biplanes. They argued that for any given weight a biplane gave more lift, and being lighter and stronger was therefore more maneuverable, the performance characteristic to which they attached the greatest importance. They did admit that a monoplane offered less head resistance because of its smaller frontal area, but they tended to treat this fact as a point of little moment.

Dowding, with his characteristic knack for getting at the heart of an issue, asked but one question: if biplanes were so superior, why had none been entered in the Schneider International Trophy competition? While biplanes had made good fighters at lower speed, there was no future for them once the Supermarine racers had set speed records that would not be surpassed for fourteen years. And Supermarine (which later became part of Vickers Aviation) went on to develop the Spitfire fighter of World War II on the technological base demonstrated in the Schneider races.[4]

Yet another Dowding anecdote underlines the importance of probing deeply by asking one more question than the experts thought to ask. In 1940 RAF fighters used .303-caliber machine guns, but it was apparent that heavier guns would be needed if German fighters added armor plate. The experts favored .50-caliber machine guns over still heavier 20-millimeter cannon. Machine guns could fire faster, carry more ammunition in their magazines, and more guns could be mounted, minimizing the risk of malfunctions. Dowding called for a test, but the experts objected. Why bother? Their trials had already shown that .50-caliber ammunition could penetrate the kind of armor plate the Germans were beginning to install in the Me–109 fighter. But Dowding insisted on a more realistic trial. He instructed the experts to install armor in a captured Me–109 and fire at the plane as if it were in the air. This time the slugs scarcely dented the armor plate. Apparently while penetrating the thin aluminum sheathing of the fuselage, the .50-caliber projectiles were robbed of their armor-piercing capability. Clearly .50-caliber machine guns alone would not be fully satisfactory against armored aircraft. Once again Dowding had demonstrated that in the quest for objectivity one must avoid leaping to seemingly obvious conclusions, as lesser minds are so often inclined to do.[5]

The cultivation of objectivity manifestly requires a persistent intellectual curiosity, a voracious desire to know more. How can one choose among alternatives if unaware of those alternatives? And finally one needs not only a sense of humor but also humility. As Oliver Cromwell said, "I beseech you, in the bowels of Christ, think it possible you may be mistaken"—good advice for all who are in danger of regarding their opinions as certainties. Or as Supreme Court Justice Oliver Wendell Holmes, Jr., once remarked, "A dead certainty is just that."

Guts, imagination, and objectivity—if these are not the full sum of essential qualities for successful command, they do afford us some convenient guides. But as always there is a catch. Like the principles of war, these three fundamental attributes so necessary for high command sometimes seem to contradict one another. Boldness and that judicious prudence required by objectivity may pull in opposite directions. The old proverb "look before you leap" is offset by that other proverb "he who hesitates is lost." One is reminded of the British artillerymen who crossed over to Belgium at the beginning of World War I. There at Le Cateau a general ordered them to set up their batteries in the open. Having been trained in the nineteenth century discipline of firing up on the line with the infantry, he apparently considered it cowardly to seek shelter behind the lines (which had become a feasible option when the new recuperator-equipped breach-loader made possible map firing or indirect fire). Needless to say, his men were promptly decimated. True, they had guts, but surely the general was lacking in both imagination and objective analysis of the tactical situation.[6]

For a more recent perception of how the mixture of guts, imagination, and objectivity is not infrequently found rather markedly skewed or unbalanced, consider an appraisal rendered on Sir Arthur "Bomber" Harris, the leader of RAF Bomber Command during World War II, by the RAF official history of the strategic air offensive against Germany:

> Sir Arthur Harris' prestige did not depend upon a reputation for good judgment. He had, after all, opposed the introduction of the incendiary technique, the creation of the Pathfinder Force, and the development of the bomb with which the Mohne and Eder dams were breached. He had confidently supposed that the Battle of Berlin could win the War, and he had declared that Bomber Command would be operationally incapable of carrying out the French railway campaign. In all of these, and in many other judgments, he had been shown to be, or at least by his superiors been supposed to be, wrong, and he had repeatedly been overruled, in theory if not always in practice. On the contrary, his prestige depended upon great acts of courage like the launching of the Thousand Bomber Raid, and, above all, upon the undying spirit with which he had mysteriously imbued the whole of Bomber Command. His great qualities, without which he would assuredly have failed in 1942, were the fearless conviction with which he approached his tasks and the single-minded courage with which he carried them out. It was his power of command and unshakable determination which distinguished him as a giant among his contemporaries. But these priceless and rare qualities inevitably found their reflections in serious and inconvenient defects.
>
> Sir Arthur Harris made a habit of seeing only one side of a question and then exaggerating it. He had a tendency to confuse advice with interference, criticism with

AIR LEADERSHIP

sabotage and evidence with propaganda. He resisted innovations and he was seldom open to persuasion. He was skeptical of the Air Staff in general and of many officers who served upon it he was openly contemptuous. Seeing all issues in black or white, he was impatient of any other possiblity, and having taken upon himself tremendous responsibilities, he expected similar powers to be conferred.[7]

Sometimes, however, all three qualities—guts, imagination, and leadership—come together in nearly perfect balance. During the summer of 1950, Gen. Douglas MacArthur in Tokyo resisted the pleas of his field commander in Korea for ever more reinforcements as the battered U.S. and South Korean forces retreated into the Pusan perimeter at the southern tip of the peninsula. MacArthur knew that his best hope of beating back the North Korean invasion was to undertake a bold stroke, an amphibious landing at Inchon behind enemy lines. MacArthur's advisers were aghast at his proposal: it was too risky; the thirty-foot tides at Inchon were a dangerous obstacle; the sea wall was too high to scale easily; there were no reinforcements available to rescue the assault team if the initial landings miscarried. But MacArthur objectively drew the fine line between foolish gamble and imaginative boldness. The operation succeeded brilliantly, sending the North Koreans into full retreat.[8] Inchon was one of the supreme moments in MacArthur's career, a time when guts, imagination, and objectivity were in a favorable balance. Weeks later, ignoring intelligence indications, MacArthur's forces were caught in a massive Chinese counterattack. So those who would study the attributes of commanders should look for the interplay of guts, imagination, and objectivity.

With this yardstick in hand, let us look into the career of General Spaatz. Although he avoided publicity and his name never became a household word, his career offers insights to students of command. He was not only the first Chief of Staff of the newly created U.S. Air Force after World War II, but during that war he was the leading Army Air Forces commander in the field and the strong right hand of AAF Commanding General "Hap" Arnold. By any criterion his career is worth scrutiny to understand the command of air forces in peace and war.

When Spaatz graduated in 1914 from the U.S. Military Academy, he stood near the middle of his class, high enough to keep out of trouble with his professors but not so high as to have missed many a good time. It is worth noting that Dwight D. Eisenhower, class of 1915, was in his cadet company. Two years after graduation, Spaatz earned his wings. He joined the First Aero Company, which was then supporting the Punitive Expedition on the Mexican Border; there General Pershing was pursuing the bandit Pancho Villa who had the temerity to shoot up Columbus, New Mexico, and kill a number of U.S. citizens. This brief adventure, limited though it was to short reconnaissance flights, made Spaatz one of the first U.S. airmen to acquire experience in combat flying. He got into military aviation on the ground floor, and in 1917 he was placed in command of the 31st Aero Squadron when it shipped to France with the American Expeditionary Force (AEF).[9]

To Spaatz's annoyance, he was not left in command of his pursuit squadron. As a major he was one of the more senior air officers in the U.S. Army, and he was ordered to take charge of the principal AEF flying training school at Issoudun. He performed effectively in this position until October 1918, just weeks before the war's end; then he received orders to return to the United States, where air officers with his range of experience were desperately needed. Instead of complying immediately with his orders, he made a side trip to the front on his own initiative and there persuaded a friend who commanded a fighter squadron to let him fly several combat missions during the Saint-Mihiel offensive. In this stay of a few days at the front he managed to shoot down three German airplanes and win a Distinguished Service Medal.[10] He returned to the United States with a reputation for guts, a reputation which would serve him in later years when, as a senior general, he was forbidden to fly against the enemy. Spaatz also brought home something else: a conviction that in all future wars winning air superiority would be an essential precondition to successful military operations by the ground forces.[11]

During the between-war years, Spaatz had a varied experience. In 1919 when Billy Mitchell organized a transcontinental air race, Spaatz was one of the first to enter. Crossing the country by airplane is now a daily routine, but in 1919 such flying was fraught with danger. On the first day of the race, crashes killed seven of the sixty-three contestants—four of them fellow Air Service officers. Spaatz not only had guts, he was a tough competitor. He would have won the west-to-east leg had he not landed at the wrong airfield. On discovering his error he took off and managed to come in twenty seconds after the winner.[12]

Again in 1929 Spaatz contributed to the stature of the fledgling air arm by breaking the world record for sustained flight, staying aloft for more than six days with an Air Corps crew in a Fokker tri-motor dubbed the *Question Mark*. This achievement not only beat the *Graf Zeppelin's* endurance record of 111 hours but demonstrated the feasibility of in-flight refueling.[13] During the flight it was necessary to take on more than two tons of fuel from the trailing hose of another plane. Fuel splashing near the flaming exhaust of three engines posed a danger of instant destruction, and at one point Spaatz was so thoroughly drenched he had to strip naked.

Spaatz commanded bombers as well as pursuit (fighters), broadening his experience as he encountered problems unique to these aircraft. He also served on evaluation boards appointed to assess the tactical suitability of

AIR LEADERSHIP

aircraft designs submitted by competing manufacturers. In these assessments imagination and objectivity were at a premium, for a decision to produce a design which subsequently proved unsatisfactory would not only waste millions of dollars but might also endanger national security.

In 1925 Spaatz attended the Air Service Tactical School, where he was exposed to instruction on air doctrine. A decade later he attended the Army's Command and General Staff College. He did so reluctantly, but any air officer who expected to achieve high rank would have to enjoy the confidence of his Army superiors. Spaatz repeated his West Point academic pattern at Fort Leavenworth, where he did nothing spectacular in the way of studies. He did, however, extend his appreciation for the problems of air-ground cooperation.[14]

Spaatz's schooling and operational assignments were interspersed with periods of staff duty. In 1933 he became Chief of Training and Operations under the Chief of Air Corps. It is his role in planning for exercises and maneuvers which gave Spaatz valuable experience handling relatively large numbers of aircraft. After war broke out in Europe in 1939, he became Chief of Plans and then Chief of the Air Staff. Clearly, here was an officer who had won the confidence of his superiors. He had demonstrated repeatedly that he was an effective officer. He had the courage to accept challenging responsibilities; he had the vision to sense appropriate solutions; he had balanced judgment. In short, Spaatz's superiors had reason to think that he had guts, imagination, and objectivity. They could entrust him with high command during a major war.

In May of 1940, just as the Phoney War (the standoff along the Franco-German frontier) became very real indeed, Spaatz was sent to France as an observer. He retreated to England with the British after Dunkirk and spent eighteen weeks there appraising the RAF in action during the Battle of Britain. It was a time when the future looked bleak for the British. Waves of German bombers pounded London and set raging fires which consumed historic landmarks. When U.S. Ambassador Joseph P. Kennedy overreacted to the blitz damage in London and predicted a German victory, Spaatz promptly cabled home a rebuttal. The Germans would not win, he pointed out, because they had failed to attain air superiority over Britain. This stand endeared Spaatz to President Roosevelt and, of course, to the leaders of the RAF.[15]

One of the entries in Spaatz's diary during his stay in London is particularly noteworthy. RAF fighter aircraft, he observed, were designed to defend Great Britain. They lacked sufficient fuel to operate effectively over the evacuation at Dunkirk. He wrote that at the very least another hour of fuel was required.[16] So the evidence is clear that when the colonel returned to the United States, he was well aware of the importance of increasing the range and endurance of fighter aircraft.

When the Japanese attack on Pearl Harbor precipitated the United States into the war, the initial plan for the air assault against Germany called for an Eighth Air Force consisting of sixteen heavy bomber groups and three pursuit groups to be deployed during 1942. The relative proportion of bombers to fighters reflected the prevailing air arm doctrine, which had been hammered out by the faculty at the Air Corps Tactical School in the between-war years. The strategic plan for the Eighth Air Force was posited upon Tactical School teachings that a sufficient number of heavy bombers with precision bombsights could destroy certain strategically critical targets and thus bring the enemy economy to the point of collapse. The assumption was that bombers could carry out their strategic mission without fighter escorts by relying largely upon tight formations, which would provide enough interlocking defensive fire to fend off enemy interceptors.[17]

Spaatz was a logical choice to command the Eighth Air Force. He had the confidence of the President, he was liked by the British, and his wide-ranging experience over the previous twenty-odd years gave assurance that he understood how to exercise command and lead men. So by July of 1942 he was back in England as a major general presiding over the painfully slow buildup of his Eighth Air Force.

As B–17 and B–24 bombers trickled into bases still under construction, RAF officers began to cast doubt on daylight bombing. They had tried it, but their losses had been so heavy that they had been compelled to switch to night bombing. They urged the Americans to do likewise. Why risk catastrophic losses? Why learn all over again at dreadful cost the lesson the RAF had already learned? Imagine Spaatz's dilemma: could he afford to ignore the British? They had the evidence of their combat experience. If he persisted and the attempt proved disastrous, all those lives lost would be charged to his bullheadedness. Here was one of those situations where guts, imagination, and objectivity all came into play.

What should a responsible commander do under the circumstances? Spaatz knew that if he shifted to night bombing, he would lose the advantage of the precision bombsight; he would have to substitute area bombing for bombing selected targets. This would mean abandoning the doctrine upon which the Eighth Air Force was conceived. The whole bomber construction program in the United States had been premised upon the number of aircraft required to eliminate carefully selected strategic targets, nodal points whose destruction could disrupt the enemy economy. There was a further complication: the supercharger exhaust pipes on U.S. bombers vented flames

AIR LEADERSHIP

below the engines, which would serve as highly visible beacons at night for German ack-ack gunners and interceptor pilots.[18]

There were a number of strong arguments which could be set against the manifest vulnerability of day bombers. Daytime operations would avoid congesting the air at night when the RAF was already operating. Targets were much easier to locate in daylight; takeoff, landing, assembly of formations aloft, and navigation were far easier; less crew training was required; and therefore the day of all-out effort would come more quickly. With U.S. crews operating by day and RAF crews by night, German interceptor crews would have no respite.[19]

So Spaatz decided there was no turning back. He dispatched his first bomber mission to Rouen on August 17, 1942, in broad daylight. This striking force and eight others which followed during the late summer and early fall returned without a single loss. Airmen were ecstatic, but their enthusiasm should have been tempered by facts. These raids were no more than shallow penetrations over the French coast. Enemy interceptors were few, because the bulk of the German air force was tied up in Russia or in North Africa. Moreover, virtually all of these strikes were heavily escorted by friendly fighters.[20]

In October 1942, for example, the Eighth Air Force mounted a 38–bomber raid over the French coast. These planes were escorted by 400 fighter aircraft, mostly British. This was a ratio of more than 10 fighters for every bomber, a sharp contrast to the doctrine implicit in the force structure of the Eighth Air Force with its ratio of 16 bomber groups to 3 fighter groups. (Given the differences in authorized strengths, this meant at full complement 768 bombers to 225 fighters or more than 3 bombers for every fighter.) Although some German fighters did manage to slip past this enormous swarm of 400 guardian escorts, they failed to shoot down any of the bombers. On the strength of this kind of performance, an Army Air Forces headquarters memo in Washington concluded that day bombers "in strong formation can be employed effectively and successfully without fighter escort."[21] Spaatz was clearly not alone in his stubborn insistence on the ability of bombers to penetrate enemy defenses. Wishful thinking and not the weight of evidence led to a dubious assertion, which resembled whistling in the dark rather than a logical inference.

Spaatz, for all his poker-playing camaraderie with his fellow officers, was in many ways a taciturn man. As he himself put it, "I never learned anything while I was talking."[22] He was not given to extended discussions, thinking out loud, or groping his way to a decision in conversations with trusted members of his staff. Nor was he one to devote much time to recording the steps by which he arrived at a decision. So one can only speculate on how long and how firmly he continued to believe that unescorted bombers could operate effectively against the enemy.

Be that as it may, the leader of the Eighth Air Force had other worries in the fall of 1942. The buildup for the North African invasion was draining away a significant fraction of the still woefully weak Eighth Air Force. It was no doubt infuriating to have to part with bomber groups so painfully brought to operational readiness, but Spaatz never complained. He sent off without protest every unit Eisenhower requested. His conduct was rewarded. Eisenhower promised to make a special point of recording for the War Department "your splendid response to every demand made on you."[23] Being mentioned favorably in dispatches to Washington was pleasing, but far more important was the solid basis of trust established between the two generals.

The diversion of units to the North African invasion imposed an inescapable delay on the buildup of the Eighth Air Force and on the day when deep penetration raids could be run against the heartland of Germany. This was so because the advocates of strategic bombing were unwilling to risk undermining the whole concept of strategic air warfare by striking with a formation too small to do the job.[24] They remembered the premature use of tanks by the British on the Somme in World War I. Delaying routine strikes deep into Germany also put off the time when Americans could learn conclusively whether unescorted bombers actually could survive in sufficient numbers to carry out their mission successfully.

As late as February 1943, for the average bomber mission the Eighth could muster only about seventy aircraft, far too few to confound the defenders with feints or to disperse their defenses with multiple thrusts. What is more, seventy aircraft were too few to achieve optimum bomb tonnages or to provide fully effective defensive fire. The drain of resources to North Africa was not the only reason why so few bombers were available. Building airfields, establishing a suitable fuel supply with all its logistical complications, training green pilots to fly in formation, and giving navigators realistic experience when impossible weather conditions grounded the whole command for days on end, all consumed far more time than anyone had anticipated.[25]

During the prolonged buildup of the Eighth Air Force, a good deal of evidence was piling up to confirm RAF assertions that day bombers would suffer unacceptable losses. As the number of bomber strikes by the Eighth gradually increased, the Germans began constructing a string of fighter bases covering the Channel coast. Improved radar made their interceptors more effective. So did their newly perfected nose attacks. Both the B–17 and the B–24 were vulnerable to attacks from directly ahead, since neither the top nor bottom turret guns covered the whole frontal area. This left only the so-called cheek guns, short-range caliber .30s with minimal striking power (fired by the bombardier from awkwardly placed flexible mounts on either side of his greenhouse) to fend off fighters with cannon boring in from dead ahead. As a consequence, even without making deep penetrations into Germany, Eighth bomber losses began to mount ominously.

In December 1942, Spaatz was given command of the Twelfth Air Force in North Africa. The respect he had won from Eisenhower (partly by loyal acceptance of the skimming of Eighth Air Force aircraft for North Africa) now paid off handsomely. Not only did Eisenhower support Spaatz in arguments with the British, but more importantly Eisenhower accepted and supported Spaatz's insistence that winning air superiority was to have absolute priority.[26]

Spaatz's concern for air superiority was clear evidence that he was not just a "bomber general." His earlier experience in fighters during World War I and the between-war years had left him with a profound conviction that air superiority was a prerequisite to all successful military operations. Thus he was prepared for Eisenhower's dismayed observation that although the Allies had 700 aircraft in North Africa compared to 500 for the Germans, every time the Germans struck they clobbered the Allied forces on the ground. Spaatz explained that the airplane was a poor defensive weapon and was largely ineffectual when scattered about in small units of dedicated air cover for ground elements; this deployment, which most ground commanders demanded, was all wrong. When the Germans attacked, they concentrated their forces and overwhelmed local air defense put up by units assigned to provide cover. The solution, Spaatz contended, was to follow the RAF example: concentrate Allied air strength and go on the offensive. This would keep German aircraft busy defending their own ground units; it would also ensure overwhelming local air superiority if the Germans did mount an attack. Eisenhower got the point; the Allied forces were concentrated and coordinated, and the Germans lost North Africa.[27]

While Spaatz was busy in the Mediteranean theater, his old friend Maj. Gen. Ira C. Eaker commanded Eighth Air Force in England. At the Casablanca Conference in January 1943, Eaker and Spaatz successfully defended American plans to bomb Germany by day while the British bombed by night—"round the clock" as Churchill put it rather too optimistically.[28]

The Combined Bomber Offensive reflected a bold and sweeping vision, but the promise of this vision reached well beyond the realities of the moment. Bomber formations of the Eighth Air Force still scarcely dared to penetrate the borders of Germany.[29] To hit the German homeland required flights of at least 250 miles, a distance well beyond the range of P-47 aircraft then available for escort duties. The P-47 originally had a combat radius of approximately 175 miles.[30] Whenever the Eighth attempted missions beyond the range of escorting fighters, the loss rate climbed sickeningly. During the first six months of 1943 when few deep penetration missions were attempted, bomber losses on each mission nonetheless ran at six or seven percent. The damage rate ranged from thirty-five percent to sixty percent, which meant that follow-up strikes often had to be delayed while repairs were carried out. The abort rate ran around forty percent attributable about equally to weather and mechanical failure.[31] Yet in April 1943 Spaatz wrote:

> I am just as convinced as ever that the operations of day bombers if applied in sufficient force . . . cannot be stopped by any means the enemy now has and . . . recent raids have gone a long way to demonstrate that fact to the more persistent unbelievers.[32]

Note how the *opinion* expressed in the first part of that sentence has become *fact* in the second. In this instance the general's faith in the strategic bomber seems to have taken precedence over his objectivity.

While asserting faith in strategic bombardment, air leaders cast about for ways and means of improving the defense of bomber formations. If fighters lacked the necessary range, why not salt each formation with "destroyer escorts," bombers without bombs but bristling with guns and protected by heavy armor. So some B–17s were modified with an extra turret, more hand-held guns, and thousands of additional rounds of ammunition. The idea of "escort destroyers" seemed a good one in theory but proved to be a flop in practice. The extra weight made the planes tail-heavy and exceedingly difficult to fly in formation. Worse yet, since they did not drop any bombs at the halfway point, the escorts were heavier on the return journey than the bombers. This forced the whole formation to throttle back to let the escorts keep up. After a few disappointing trials, the experiment was abandoned. Here was a case of a lively imagination at work in conceiving a scheme but a lack of objectivity in thinking it through.[33]

By July of 1943 it was becoming evident that British predictions were all too true; unescorted bombers were taking prohibitive losses. A raid on Hamburg suffered a twelve percent loss. A raid against Kassel lost twenty-three percent; another strike, against Kiel, lost fourteen percent.[34] By this time some American air leaders were no longer so confident that they could carry out their strategic mission. Losses were beginning to run ahead of replacements. The Schweinfurt raids in August and October 1943 suffered twenty-six-percent and thirty-three-percent losses.[35] The latter figure came close to the forty percent casualties of the infamous Charge of the Light Brigade; and what air arm commander wanted to go down in history as "someone who'd blundered"?

When Eisenhower returned to England from the Mediterranean theater and took his place as Supreme Allied Commander to plan for the invasion of

AIR LEADERSHIP

Europe, he took Spaatz with him. Eisenhower had already expressed his high opinion of Spaatz for the latter's unselfish cooperation in supporting diversions from the Eighth Air Force to North Africa, but after working with him there, his esteem was even greater. Eisenhower saw "no better all-round Air officer than Spaatz. . . . I wouldn't trade him for any other field commander of the Air Forces that I know." By the end of the war, the Supreme Commander put Spaatz on a par with Gen. Omar N. Bradley as the number one general in his command; in Eisenhower's words, Spaatz was "experienced and able . . . loyal and cooperative; modest and selfless."[36]

Given Eisenhower's appraisal, it is scarcely surprising that Spaatz received the appointment as commander of the United States Strategic Air Forces in Europe (USSTAF), which was to coordinate the strategic bombing operations of Eighth Air Force based in Britain and Fifteenth Air Force based in Italy. This task was complicated by repeated calls from ground force commanders desperately in need of air support. Although the Combined Chiefs of Staff had assigned top priority to the Combined Bomber Offensive, they did allow for "emergency" diversions of bombers from strategic objectives (such as the German aircraft industry and synthetic oil production facilities) to support ground operations.[37]

In February 1944, for example, Spaatz was organizing a massive assault on German aircraft factories when the situation at the Anzio beachhead in Italy turned critical. During the German offensive of February 16–19, Fifteenth Air Force bombers had to focus their attention on Anzio. This was typical of the dilemmas confronting Spaatz. If he released bombers in Italy from their share of strategic attacks on Germany, German fighters could concentrate on the bomber stream approaching from Britain. In the case of Anzio, the dilemma was resolved by Germany's bad weather which did not clear until February 20th. By then the German offensive had spent itself, and Fifteenth Air Force bombers were available to join Eighth Air Force in the "Big Week" bombing of Germany.[38]

By the time Spaatz took over the USSTAF, the problem of high loss rates for bombers was already well on its way toward solution. The answer lay in providing fighter escorts all the way to the target and back, a feat made possible by the addition of droppable fuel tanks. A P–47 with a mere 175-mile combat radius using internal fuel could increase this to 325 miles by adding a 108–gallon drop tank. Increased internal tankage along with droppable wing and belly tanks gave the P–47 an operating radius of a thousand miles, more than enough to go all the way to Berlin and back. Adding drop tanks to the P–51 Mustang and the P–38 Lightning gave them even greater ranges. Using escorts all the way in and back would permit Eighth Air Force to cut its heavy bomber losses to about one percent by October 1944.[39]

28

In early 1944 at long last the way was open for a full-fledged test of bomber doctrine with enough bombers to achieve critical mass. The Combined Bomber Offensive could now begin in earnest on the seventy-six selected precision targets identified as vital. These targets were in the following categories: submarine assembly yards, aircraft assembly plants, ball bearing factories, oil refineries, synthetic rubber plants, and military vehicle factories. But in Spaatz's eyes, the real objective was the fighter strength of the German air force. He rightly reasoned that hitting the selected targets would force enemy fighters to come up in defense. This would give Allied escorts the opportunity to chew up German fighter strength and thus win that air superiority which was so essential. Once air superiority had been achieved, an Allied invasion across the beaches of Normandy could begin and strategic bombers could roam over enemy cities with virtual impunity.[40]

Just as a suitable team of bombers and escorts became available to carry out the strategic offensive on an adequate scale, the Supreme Commander insisted in March 1944 on switching USSTAF assets to his personal control. Eisenhower wanted them to concentrate on supporting Operation Overlord, the Normandy invasion—initially by interdiction bombing of the rail network and other transportation elements in France and later by rendering direct tactical support to the invading troops. General Spaatz loyally acceded to Eisenhower's call but not without misgivings.[41]

Spaatz was quite willing to concede that his strategic bombers should be used to assist Operation Overlord by interdicting enemy routes to the beachhead, but he felt this effort should be limited to a very short period immediately prior to D-day. His reasoning reflected a good deal of imagination in assessing the problem. So long as USSTAF bombers continued to pound vital targets in the heartland of Germany, the German fighters could be counted on to come up and fight. This would give Allied escorts an opportunity to consume them now that the advantage of numbers was passing to the attackers. Moreover, as the bombers continued to hit aircraft factories and oil refineries, the capacity of the Germans to replace losses and sustain an effective force would decline. Further, by hitting targets deep in Germany, USSTAF bombers would compel the enemy to retain most of his fighter strength at bases in the homeland, far from the invasion area. This would leave them ill-situated to respond to the invasion threat when it ultimately came. Finally, Spaatz reasoned, the Germans would not be inclined to defend the French rail net with the same zeal they displayed in protecting their own vital centers. While attacks on the transportation network in France might interdict the invasion area, they would not induce so many German fighters to rise; thus USSTAF would be thwarted in its effort to achieve air superiority.

AIR LEADERSHIP

Despite the clarity of Spaatz's reasoning and his persistence in presenting his case, the Supreme Commander insisted on taking charge of the bombers and concentrating on the interdiction role in France. Thus for a period of no less than four months, at a time when USSTAF was in prime condition to carry out its strategic mission, its assets were diverted to the execution of a tactical role. Even after D-day when it looked as if the way was at last clear for Spaatz to regain control of the bombers, they continued to be used against V–1 missile sites where the Germans launched the low-cost pilotless aircraft from concrete ramps along the English Channel. Not until September 1944 did USSTAF get back to an all-out strategic bombardment effort, although Eisenhower had allowed some such missions to be undertaken during his period of tactical control, especially when the weather seemed too good not to bomb strategic targets.[42]

The results achieved by American bombers, despite their prolonged diversion to tactical use, were impressive. By the end of the war they had dropped more than half a million tons of bombs on Germany.[43] What is more, they had played a vital role in neutralizing the German air force and achieving air superiority. By hitting oil targets, the bombers reduced German flying training time and thus made German fighters easier to shoot down; by hitting aircraft plants, the bombers forced dispersion which limited production; and by attracting German interceptors, the bombers gave escort fighters opportunities for air-to-air victories. The Allies gained unquestioned air superiority. There was no effective German air effort to hinder the Normandy landings.[44] Indeed, as Lt. Gen. Baron Geyr von Schweppenburg expressed it, the Allies achieved not merely "air superiority" but "air mastery."[45]

When the United States Strategic Bombing Survey submitted its voluminous reports after the war, the survey analysts concluded that Allied air power had been "decisive." This did not mean that air power or strategic bombardment could have won the war alone.[46] One can deduce that Spaatz, as a major actor in this great drama, deserved a share of credit for the results achieved. History has accorded him that credit, which he no doubt richly deserved. But those who study the art of command should take pains to look beyond success to the mistakes made, the wrong turnings or unfortunate choices, and try to learn from them. Doing this in no way diminishes the stature of the individuals studied. Indeed, analysis of a commander's mistakes will almost certainly make us more appreciative of the difficulties, the unknowns, and the uncertainties which beset him at every important turn in the road.

Looking back with the perspective of the historian, it is obvious that extending the range of fighter aircraft so they could escort bombers to the most distant targets was vital to the success of strategic bombardment. And it was drop tanks which made possible this extended range. If drop tanks made a crucial difference, one may well ask, why were they not employed much earlier? Why were there no long-range fighter escorts in 1942? Had they been available, the Combined Bomber Offensive would have been better equipped for strategic bombardment in 1943. There would have been a more adequate test for the concept of strategic bombardment much sooner. Such a test might have reduced the scale and duration of the invasion by ground forces—even if bombing could not entirely obviate that effort (as some enthusiasts in the bomber community had suggested might be possible).

Historical investigation of the drop tank problem has uncovered a number of curious facts. Way back in 1922 when Spaatz was a major commanding the First Pursuit Group, he declared that bombers should be escorted by pursuit aircraft with a range at least equal to that of bombers.[47] This notion of long-range fighters was not just a pipe dream. In 1924 Billy Mitchell urged a similar course and asserted that the Air Service was actually attaining the necessary range for pursuit planes "by means of auxiliary tanks which can be dropped."[48] By the time long-range, four-engine bombers had become a reality in the late 1930s, however, Spaatz appears to have lost interest in the use of escort fighters with the necessary range.

The conventional wisdom among aircraft designers was that a lightweight fighter, being more maneuverable, would always whip a heavier fighter of the sort required to achieve a combat radius of more than 500 miles. But a heavier fighter implied one designed to provide massive *internal* tankage. This ignored the potential of the drop tank which could enhance the range of a fighter without substantially increasing its intrinsic weight.[49]

Spaatz's stand on the drop tank issue was revealed in a document he signed in March 1941 when serving as Chief of the Plans Division in the Office of the Chief of the Air Corps. At that time a proposal had come in urging the use of external fuel tanks on fighter aircraft to increase their combat range. Spaatz disapproved the idea, saying: "It is believed that" providing additional range would be "incompatible with the mission of pursuit." Adding drop tanks, he continued, would "provide opportunities for improper tactical use of pursuit types."[50]

The very language of this memo is revealing. Note the phrase "it is believed that," a construction much employed by staff officers. It expresses an opinion, not a fact. And just who does the believing is left vague. While Spaatz signed the document and therefore accepted responsibility for its contents, the memo was drafted by one of his staff whose initials were on the

AIR LEADERSHIP

file copy: Hoyt S. Vandenberg, the officer who some years later would follow Spaatz as Chief of Staff of the newly formed postwar Air Force.

Only a short while before writing the memo on drop tanks, Vandenberg had been an instructor in the Pursuit Branch of the Air Corps Tactical School. His lectures are still available. Instead of reworking and updating the lectures he inherited from Capt. Claire Chennault, Vandenberg simply used the same texts over and over again more or less unchanged. He recited the litany of characteristics which had become accepted wisdom in the 1930s: superior speed, rate of climb, and service ceiling. Operational range was not even mentioned as a desirable characteristic, although there was a passing reference to "endurance" as desirable in those pursuits to be used when flying continuous air alerts and coastal patrols.[51]

Clearly Vandenberg's reaction to the drop tank proposal was a rote response. He failed to conceptualize the problem of the fighter as escort. Instead, he simply articulated the conventional wisdom on fighter aircraft as weapons dedicated to air superiority or to local interception of incoming bombers. And in so doing he led his superior, Spaatz, into a most unfortunate decision. What Vandenberg seems to have carried away from the Air Corps Tactical School was dogma, a doctrinal position which he applied by rote at a time when the circumstances had changed and a new solution was required.

Spaatz's failure appears more surprising than Vandenberg's when one realizes that Spaatz decided against drop tanks *after* returning from his extended stay as an observer in England. He made his decision against drop tanks after he had learned from his RAF friends about the acute vulnerability of heavily armed bombers, even those with gun turrets. What is more, he recommended against drop tanks after he himself had written from England that fighters there had lacked range and that tankage should be added to provide at least one more hour of flying time.[52] Spaatz's veto on drop tanks is still more difficult to understand in light of the fact that the Japanese had been using drop tanks in operational units ever since 1938. Zero fighters equipped with such tanks in the summer of 1940 accompanied Japanese bombers all the way to Chungking, a round trip of over a thousand miles.[53] Why were this performance and its obvious implications ignored?

There are a number of factors in this equation which can be cited in extenuation. It is deceptively easy to read history backwards. We now know that American fighter aircraft—the P–38, the P–47, the P–51—ultimately were to prove fully capable of meeting German propeller-driven aircraft on their own terms. But in 1941 this was not at all evident. Each of these fighters was in the early stages of development; each had bugs which had to be eliminated. As long as Spaatz and his subordinates were uncertain about the ability of American fighters to outmaneuver their German opponents in combat, they were exceedingly reluctant to add any weight or protuberances which might impair fighter performance.[54]

Even after the decision was finally made to go ahead with drop tanks (a decision made without Spaatz who was in North Africa), there were other delays and complications. Each type of aircraft required a drop tank designed to suit its peculiar needs. Tanks could shift a plane's center of gravity or slow down its acceleration dangerously. If fighters were to engage the enemy at altitudes above 20,000 feet, pumps were required to extract fuel from low-slung drop tanks. With pumps, plumbing, valves, release shackles, and external pylons, one type of tank involved 159 parts turned out by 43 manufacturers. Technical problems delayed initial deliveries, but technical problems could be resolved in due course once the basic decision to use drop tanks had been made.[55]

The real problem was not technical but conceptual. And this leads one back to Spaatz, the man of whom Eisenhower said, "I wouldn't trade him for any other field commander of the Air Forces that I know."[56] Against the measuring rod of guts, imagination, and objectivity, how did Spaatz stack up as a commander? Of guts there can be no question. Physical courage, moral courage, character, loyalty—these he had in full measure. But these qualities can produce a stubborn, wrongheaded response to a changing reality, if they are not balanced by imagination and objectivity. Spaatz sometimes displayed imagination and objectivity. As illustrated by his campaign against oil targets, he could envision large schemes and pursue the necessary details to carry them out. In the case of drop tanks, however, he made an unimaginative decision in 1941 that would prove costly in 1943. His failure to imagine the need for long-range fighter escorts may have been grounded in his lack of objectivity about bombers. Like many other air leaders, he had invested so much of his faith in bombers that he underestimated their vulnerability.

It is unlikely that any commander has been able to maintain perfect objectivity about his current situation or imagine fully his future predicament. Each commander has looked outward through his preconceptions. That is not all bad. Without doctrine to structure reality, a commander would have difficulty reacting effectively in a crisis. But doctrine should be constantly under scrutiny so that it is based on the best information available; otherwise doctrine may become dogma.

If a leader of Spaatz's caliber could occasionally be crippled by a lack of objectivity, we can be sure that the problem has been widespread. Those who would study Spaatz's career for insights on what makes a commander effective would do well not to be blinded by the indubitable success of this able master of air power to the point of ignoring his mistakes. In the case of

AIR LEADERSHIP

fighter drop tanks and bomber vulnerability, how should one account for the general's lapse from objectivity? Was it some intrinsic trait of personality? Was it a rather casual attitude toward hard study? Was it some defect in the curriculum of the military educational institutions he attended, some failure to develop his sensitivity to the requirements of a rigorous objectivity? Or would the best academic preparation have proved inadequate against the bomber's seductive promise of an independent air force? Any officer who expects to benefit by studying the historical record will have to begin by learning to formulate for himself questions such as these, for only they can carry him beyond the surface narrative of events in a leader's life.

Notes

1. Hugh Gibson, ed., *The Ciano Diaries, 1939–1943* (Garden City, New York, 1946), pp 302 and 314–15.
2. R. V. Jones, *Most Secret War* (London, 1978), p 106.
3. See introduction to 1953 edition of Forester's *The General* for comments on German reactions.
4. Basil Collier, *Leader of the Few: The Authorized Biography of Air Chief Marshal, the Lord Dowding of Bentley Priory* (London, 1957), p 146; Peter Wykeham, *Fighter Command* (London, 1960), p 61.
5. Collier, pp 202–3.
6. Robert H. Scales, "Artillery in Small Wars: The Evolution of British Artillery Doctrine, 1860–1914" (Dissertation, Duke, 1976), pp 307–10.
7. Sir Charles Webster and Noble Frankland, *The Strategic Air Offensive Against Germany* (London, 1961), III, 80.
8. Roy E. Appleman, *South to the Naktong, North to the Yalu* [US Army in the Korean War] (Washington, 1961).
9. The best brief sketch of Spaatz is by Alfred Goldberg in Michael Carver, ed., *The War Lords* (Boston, 1976), pp 568–81. David Mets is writing a full length biography under the auspices of the Air Force Historical Foundation. See also War Department biographical release on Spaatz in USAF Historical Research Center (AFHRC), Maxwell AFB, Ala., K141.2421–Spaatz–1919–74.
10. War Department General Order 123, Dec 11, 1918; *New York Times*, Jan 13, 1929, p IX–12.
11. Intvw, USAF Academy history department with Spaatz, Sep 27, 1968, AFHRC K239.0512–583.
12. *New York Times*, Oct 9, 1919, p 1; Oct 12, p 3.
13. *New York Times*, Jan 13, 1929, p IX–12.
14. Jon Reynolds, "Education and Training for High Command: General Hoyt S. Vandenberg's Early Career" (Dissertation, Duke, 1980), pp 173–75.
15. Carl Spaatz, "Leaves from my Battle of Britain Diary," *Airpower Historian* 4 (Apr 57), 6; Spaatz, "Strategic Air Power," *Foreign Affairs* 24 (Apr 46), 387; Goldberg, p 569; Ira C. Eaker, "As I Remember Them," *Aerospace Historian* 20 (Winter 73), 195.
16. Spaatz, "Battle of Britain Diary," p 68.
17. Thomas H. Greer, *The Development of Air Doctrine in the Army Air Arm, 1917–1941* (USAF Historical Study 89, Maxwell AFB, Ala., 1955), pp 152–55. Sixteen heavy bomber groups involved 768 aircraft; 3 pursuit groups involved 225 aircraft. See pp 1–5 of "Plan for Bomber Command" (Eighth Air Force), Miscellaneous Papers of Gen. Ira Eaker, Feb-Aug 1942, AFHRC 520.168–1.
18. "Plan for Bomber Command."
19. "History of Early Days in England," report of Special Observer Board in London headed by Maj Gen J.E. Chaney, p 56, Maj Gen C.L. Bolté Collection, 1917–1930s, US Army Military History Institute, Carlisle Barracks, Penn.
20. W. F. Craven and J. L. Cate, *The Army Air Forces in World War II* (Chicago, 1949), II, 233–34.
21. Craven and Cate, II, 222. See also intvw, Thomas A. Sturm and Hugh N. Ahman, USAF Oral History Program, with Gen Laurence S. Kuter, USAF Ret, Sep 30–Oct 3, 1974, p 114, AFHRC K239.0512–810.
22. Ira Eaker, "General Carl A. Spaatz, USAF," *Air Force*, Sep 74, p 44.

AIR LEADERSHIP

23. Alfred D. Chandler, ed., *The Papers of Dwight David Eisenhower: The War Years* (Baltimore: Johns Hopkins, 1970), II, 703. See also intvw, Bruce Hopper with Spaatz, Jun 27, 1945, Spaatz Collection, AFHRC 519.1612-2/1943-5.
24. Craven and Cate, II, 237.
25. *Ibid*, p 308.
26. Hopper intvw with Spaatz.
27. Kuter intvw, pp 277, 292. Kuter credits RAF Air Vice Marshal Sir Arthur Coningham of the Western Desert Air Force in North Africa with the genesis of this idea. See also Richard H. Kohn and Joseph P. Harahan, eds., *Air Superiority in World War II and Korea* (Washington, DC, 1983), pp 32-33; Sir Arthur Coningham, "The Development of Tactical Air Forces," *Journal of the United Service Forces* 9 (1946), 211-27; I. C. Eaker, "As I Remember Them . . ." *Aerospace Historian* 20 (Winter 73), 196.
28. DeWitt S. Copp, *Forged in Fire: Strategy and Decision in the Air War over Europe, 1940-45* (Garden City, New York, 1982), p 351.
29. Goldberg, p 571.
30. Draft report for Spaatz, "U.S. Strategic Air Forces in World War II," Part I, Vol II, Air Force Historical Div, 1947, AFHRC 106-90.
31. William Emerson, "Doctrine and Dogma: Operation Pointblank as Case History," *Army* 13 (Jun 63), 54; Craven and Cate, II, 260-62.
32. Bernard L. Boylan, *Development of the Long-Range Escort Fighter* (USAF Historical Study 136, Maxwell AFB, Ala., 1955), p 86. See also B. L. Boylan, "The Search for a Long-Range Escort Plane," *Military Affairs* 30 (Summer 66), 57-67.
33. Stephen P. Birdsall, "The Destroyer Escorts," *Airpower Historian* 12 (Jul 65), 92-94.
34. Boylan, *Development*, p 90.
35. *Ibid*, p 97.
36. Chandler, IV, 2129 and 2466.
37. Spaatz statement, HQ USSTAF, Jan 4, 1945, AFHRC 519.9512-1.
38. Craven and Cate, III, 30-32, 327-28.
39. Boylan, *Development*, p 135; Eaker Report on Eighth Air Force (Feb 20, 1942 to Dec 31, 1943), Dec 31, 1943, AFHRC 168.61-3; *Army Air Forces Statistical Digest: World War II* (Washington: AAF Office of Statistical Control, Dec 1945), pp 221 and 255.
40. Spaatz, "Strategic Bombing," in *Ten Eventful Years: 1937-1946* (Chicago: Encycl. Britannica, 1947), p 180. See also J.F. Loosbrock, "A Sense of What Would Work," *Air Force*, Sep 74, p 53.
41. Maj Gen Haywood S. Hansell, Jr., *The Air Plan that Defeated Hitler* (Atlanta, 1972), pp 186-92.
42. *Ibid*, p 191.
43. *Army Air Forces Statistical Digest: World War II*, p 240.
44. Spaatz to Arnold, Report on Goering Interrogation, May 23, 1945, AFHRC 519.1612-2(1943-4); Spaatz, "Strategic," pp 176-81; David MacIsaac, *Strategic Bombing in World War Two* (New York, 1976), pp 76-77; notes for a Spaatz press conference, 1945, AFHRC 519.9512-1(1945).
45. A.F. Wilt, "Normandy in a Different Key," *Air University Review* 34 (July 1983), 104.
46. *The United States Strategic Bombing Survey: Summary Report (European War)*, Washington, Sep 30, 1945, p 15.
47. Boylan, *Development*, p 9.
48. Quoted in Maj R.L. Swedenburg, "In Search of an Environment for the Growth of Space Doctrine," (paper for AFA Space Symposium, Apr 1-3, 1981), ACSC, Maxwell AFB, Ala., Dec 80, p 12.
49. Boylan, *Development*, pp 35-36.
50. Memo, Chief Plans Div, Office Chief of Air Corps, for Exec., Mar 10, 1941, AFHRC reel A1422, frame B86-7. For the views of contemporaries on Chennault's thinking, see Hansell, p 19; Kuter intvw, III, 113-14; intvw, USAF Academy with Maj Gen Haywood Hansell, Jr., Apr 19, 1967, pp 22-26, AFHRC K239.0512-629.

51. Air Corps Tactical School, pursuit aviation course texts for 1937, 1938, and 1939–40, AFHRC 248.101-8.

52. Spaatz, "Battle of Britain Diary," p 68.

53. Rene J. Francillon, *Japanese Aircraft of the Pacific War* (London, 1970), p 345; Mastatake Okumiya and Jiro Horikoshi, *Zero!* (New York, 1956), pp 32–33; Jiro Horikoshi, *Eagles of Mitsubishi* (Seattle, 1981), pp 125–27. The author is indebted to Dr. John F. Guilmartin, Jr., of Rice University for calling his attention to the Japanese use of drop tanks as early as 1938. See also Capt. C.S. Shershun, "The Man Who Downed Colin Kelly," *Aerospace Historian* 13 (Winter 66), 149–50, in which leading Zero pilot Saburo Sakai recalls flying for as much as twelve hours over Formosa. See also Williamson Murray, *Strategy for Defeat: The Luftwaffe, 1933–1945* (Maxwell AFB, Ala.,1983), pp 48–49, which mentions Condor Legion use of drop tanks in Spain during the Civil War to get 125 miles of range.

54. Boylan, *Development*, p 133.

55. Hist, Eighth Air Force Service Command, 1942–43, Chapter 5, "Materiel and Supplies," pp 60–63, AFHRC 519.01; Air Technical Service Command case histories: "Droppable Fuel Tanks, 1939–1943," AFHRC 202.2–6, and "Fighter Airplane Range Extension Program," AFHRC 202.2–11.

56. Chandler, IV, 2129.

Discussion

Brig. Gen. Brian S. Gunderson, USAF, Retired, chair
Gen. Mark E. Bradley, Jr., USAF, Retired
Dr. Alfred Goldberg
Dr. I. B. Holley, Jr., Maj. Gen., USAFR, Retired
Gen. Curtis E. LeMay, USAF, Retired
Dr. David R. Mets, Lt. Col., USAF, Retired

Holley: What is our purpose here? Many of us in this gathering have tried our hand at the anatomy of command, trying to discern what the essentials are. I suppose almost everyone who has tried it has found it to be an almost impossible task. After all, the factors that make a successful commander are inescapably beyond recovery since they largely stem from motivation, and most historians agree that we will never be able to get at men's motivations. Nevertheless, we try.

One of the ingredients of a successful commander that we discover is that he listens and he engages in the dialectic process. He learns as he goes along. I guess what we are saying, especially to the younger people in the audience (not only today's commanders but the would-be commanders), is that one should read biographies even though you know the biographers are not getting everything there is to get—they are not finding all the clues, and they are not discerning all the passages. Perhaps the most important ones have been missed.

I hope General LeMay will tell us how he went about producing an autobiography in the as-told-to mode.*

LeMay: As I neared the end of my service, I had made up my mind that I was going to be one general who didn't write a book. But when that news got around, many of my friends immediately descended on me and pointed out that by a chain of circumstances I had been present during a lot of significant events. I finally gave in and said, "All right, but I don't have any writing talent at all. I can't even write a letter to my wife. I will only do it if I can find somebody to actually do the writing."

After thinking it over a while, I finally settled on MacKinlay Kantor. I had read some of his stuff before the war. Lo and behold when I arrived in

---

*Curtis E. LeMay with MacKinlay Kantor, *Mission with LeMay* (New York, 1965).

AIR LEADERSHIP

England, I found him as a freelance war correspondent living with my ground echelon, the 305th. He was there when I left and went on to the 3d Division. After the war he was in and out of Strategic Air Command from time to time. When the Korean fracas came along, he went to Korea with one of the B-29 groups and wrote a couple of books on that subject over there. So he knew a lot of the story.

I went down to see him one day in Florida where he was living. He said he would like to do it, but he had just had a heart attack and his doc had forbidden him to do any work. I talked to a couple of other people without much success and was about to drop the whole subject, when Mac came through my office in the Pentagon and said: "I have just been to New York to see my publisher, and I have a new doc; he has thrown all the pills away except one and I can go back to work. When do we start?" We sat down and sort of made an outline of the chapters we were going to have and then a little more detailed outline of each of the chapters. Mac said: "I never write a book in chronological order; that would drive me crazy. I just skip around. Is that all right with you?" I said, "Okay, anyway you want to do it."

If they predicted we weren't going to have a flap, he would show up and spend the weekend with a tape recorder and notes. As I say, he knew a lot of the story too. So we both talked into the tape recorder. He would go home and write something double-spaced on yellow note pads and send it up to me. I would throw it in the drawer, and when I could get to it, I would read it over and make a note or two, saying, "No, I remember it this way," or "No, you can't say that; I don't want to say that." He was more for giving McNamara a working over than I thought was really appropriate for me to do at the time.

This was started a couple of years before I retired. After I retired, I went down to Florida and spent some time with him down there, and we finished it up. By and large I think he did pretty well, although I missed a few things in the reading that I wish I had caught, like this bombing back into the Stone Age business.* That sort of gave me the reputation of being somebody whose solution to every problem was bombing hell out of them. That's not my idea of the solution to every problem. But by and large I think he did pretty well. I was happy with it.

Holley: One other point I should like to raise with General LeMay this

---

*Mission with LeMay, p 565, discusses the best way to stop the North Vietnamese from interfering in South Vietnam: "My solution to the problem would be to tell them frankly that they've got to draw in their horns and stop their aggression, or we're going to bomb them back into the Stone Age." To convince the North Vietnamese that the United States "really meant business," General LeMay proposed conventional bombing or mining of North Vietnam's ports, ground transportation, fuel, and industry. "Apply whatever force it is necessary to employ to stop things quickly. The main thing is *stop it*. The quicker you stop it, the more lives you save."

afternoon stems directly from Colonel Mets's presentation. General Spaatz was terribly concerned about range extension: all those aircraft coming back from the Continent with rapidly emptying tanks. It always has fascinated me that he did not, as far as we know from the record, attempt air-to-air refueling. Given the fact that he was the hero of the *Question Mark*, the refueling in 1929, was there no experimenting with air-to-air refueling at least on the homeward leg, crossing the Channel, when you were down to that last cupful of fuel?

LeMay: No, there wasn't any of that at all. But remember the circumstances at the time. The first mission with B–17s over the Continent was, I think, the Fourth of July 1942, and about a half dozen of them got off. We were building an air force. We didn't have any bombers, let alone any tankers to carry gasoline for them. So it was necessary to get the bombers over there, not complicate the problem by demanding tankers when we didn't have enough bombers to go even a short distance. It was building the force. That doesn't mean they didn't think about range. For instance, the B–17s I got in the 3d Division, which was the last one formed over there, had longer range tanks than the models before. We were doing something about it. The P–51 came along, and General Bradley can tell you more about that. He was at Dayton and was responsible for adding the range to the P–51.* So there was something being done about that, but not to the point of demanding a new airplane to extend the range, because we didn't have the airplanes to go in the first place. Mark, do you want to amplify on that?

Bradley: I think that is right. I agree completely. There really hadn't been any technical development of refueling that I know of done in the United States since the *Question Mark*. Maybe there had, but I didn't know about it. The first refueling system I saw was a British system developed after the war in 1948. We went and got it, and they sent me down to Wichita to put it into the B–29s. A Boeing engineer and I got together and invented the boom that Curt still likes.

LeMay: I hesitate to add anything to this splendid paper that Colonel Mets has written, since I only served directly under General Spaatz for about two weeks. So the bulk of my knowledge is hearsay except for this two-week period, and that won't take long to run over although I might go into it pretty much in detail.

After the war was over in Europe, the Combined Chiefs, I gather, decided that they would launch a big air campaign against Japan. They would organize the strategic air forces of the Pacific. The B–29s would be an

---

*See Mark E. Bradley, "The P–51 over Berlin," *Aerospace Historian*, Sep 74, pp 125–28. Bradley suggested adding an internal fuel tank behind the pilot's seat; together with wing drop tanks, the new internal tank gave the P–51 enough range to fly from England to Berlin and back.

AIR LEADERSHIP

American contribution, plus the Eighth Air Force with their B–17s, which would move into the Philippines and Okinawa from Europe; the RAF would be over there, too, under Sir Hugh Lloyd. I was notified that this reorganization was going to take place and I was to be chief of staff of a new command.

General Spaatz arrived out in the Marianas a couple of weeks before the war actually ended. The first thing he did when he got off the airplane was hand me a letter. It was a letter from President Truman authorizing us to drop the first atomic bomb. I told General Spaatz that the 509th had been there for a lengthy time and I had put them into a training program immediately. Most of their crews had had actual missions to Japan, and they were ready to go. As far as I knew, the date for dropping the first bomb, 6 August, hadn't changed. We had not made a choice of targets yet, because that would depend on the weather at the time. He nodded at that.

I then gave him a briefing on the command and took him around to show him what we were doing. That took a couple of days. He sent a message off to General Arnold stating that he, Spaatz, had had a chance to look over the B–29 operations and he thought it was the best organized and the most technically proficient organization in history to date. That convinced me he had a little confidence in me, and he told me to organize his staff. He brought about a half dozen people with him so I asked him if he had any preferences or any suggestions on the staff, and he said no. I said, "Well, I don't know the people that you brought out here. I do know the people that are here. I will probably lean pretty heavily on the people that are out here. That might lead to a little trouble with General Twining when he arrives." Spaatz said, "Well, we will worry about that later. Go ahead."

Actually I only got a couple of people chosen. I think I had one quonset hut with a couple of desks and chairs and got Tommy Power, one of my wing commanders, down to be operations officer. General Twining came out and relieved me. So I started to get things in line to get some buildings and a place to house us, but before I made much more of a move, the war was over.

I never got any direct orders from General Spaatz on anything. We met mostly at the poker table. We had three or four poker games in that two weeks. I knew somehow what he wanted at the end of that time. It seems to me that is mostly the way he operated. I had frequent contact with him after the war, of course, on fishing trips and so on. He liked to give people the impression that he was lazy. Even in the middle of crises, he would turn things over to somebody else and say, "I will be down at the club; call me if you need me." It seems to me that he got people to be around him that he had all the confidence in the world in, people for whom he didn't have to draw a picture every time he wanted something done. He set the goal and let them get busy and get it done, and they did.

Goldberg: I have been convinced by Colonel Mets that Spaatz was not the model of a modern major general or any other general for that matter, so I don't know whether he is a model for air leadership or any other leadership. It would have helped to know just what a model is and how air leadership differs from other leadership, and perhaps we can say something about that later on, or somebody will say something about that.

I can only say that, as a result of some personal observations of Spaatz during and after World War II and considerable study of his papers and other materials dealing with him, I formed some strong impressions about him that I believe are supported by a good deal of evidence as well as by my own subjective reactions. The question to be addressed perhaps ought to be: what were the most important traits that distinguished Spaatz as a military leader and may have contributed to his success in that role? This is especially appropriate for Spaatz because I have the impression that among the top military leaders of World War II, or almost any other time for that matter, he was *sui generis*, truly unique. He represented a composite of characteristics, as Colonel Mets has brought out very well, that I find very unusual among military commanders. I am sure that other commanders had unusual combinations of traits—that many were unique in their own ways. It's just that I found Spaatz *more* unique than others, if you will pardon the use of the comparative in the sense that some are more equal than others.

First, and something that is often overlooked but very widely known, he had a good sense of humor about himself as well as about others. The importance of this is difficult to exaggerate, for self-humor is a form of objectivity. It meant that he had the capacity to see things in proportion; it meant that he could relax, that he could see the absurdities of life about him even in the most serious situations. A sense of humor can indeed be a saving grace, in fact a lifesaver for people under great stress. Robert Lovett[*] (who knew Spaatz very well and had a grand sense of humor himself) was a great admirer of Spaatz and not least of his sense of humor, which Lovett once described as zaney. Lovett remarked of James Forrestal, the first Secretary of Defense and a close friend, that he probably would not have succumbed to the stresses and strains of office had he had a sense of humor.[+] It was a tragic lack, as indeed it is for anyone who doesn't have it.

---

[*]Robert A. Lovett (1895–1986) was Assistant Secretary of War for Air, 1941–45; he later served as Secretary of Defense during the Korean War.

[+]Two months after resigning as Secretary of Defense, James Forrestal (1892–1949) plunged to his death from a window of the Bethesda Naval Medical Center in the Maryland suburbs of Washington; he had been suffering from severe depression.

AIR LEADERSHIP

Colonel Mets referred to Spaatz's lack of ambition. I think this is true in the sense of being driven by the desire for self-advancement. He was not driven by that desire. He was ambitious for the institutions he served: the Air Service, the Air Corps, the Army Air Forces, and finally the U.S. Air Force. Because he was not personally ambitious, he was not a toady or a sycophant to any man, be it his immediate superiors, chiefs of staff, prime ministers, or presidents. Accordingly, as Mets said, he was not a hypocrite or a double-talker. He was forthright and up front, and there is a great deal of testimony to that effect. He was essentially a modest man, indifferent to and indeed avoiding personal publicity. He was informal, unpretentious, and even unmilitary in his manner at times. He had the self-confidence that comes from being one's own man, from being secure in who and what he was. George Patton said that all very successful commanders are prima donnas and must be so treated. He could not possibly have had Spaatz in mind.

There was one characteristic of Spaatz that was neither innate nor acquired. Colonel Mets has also referred to this in passing. Spaatz cannot claim credit for this although some people are more favored by it than others. He was lucky. He had the good fortune to be in the right place at the right time during the later years of his career. He was in the Office of the Chief of Air Corps and in the Headquarters Army Air Forces under his friend and admirer, Hap Arnold, at the right time to hold important positions, to get promoted to brigadier general and major general, and then get the choice assignment as Commanding General of the Eighth Air Force. From then on he was always in the right place. There was logic in it too, but also a continuing element of luck. This is the element of chance in history that we find so difficult to take account of in explaining what happened and why.

Let me speak finally of his relationship with Hap Arnold, which has also been alluded to and which was, once again, unique, and no other officer, I believe, in the Army Air Forces has enjoyed such a relationship. Arnold regarded Spaatz as his peer and it seems, on occasion, even more than a peer. Certainly Spaatz treated Arnold more as a peer than a superior during the war. This could only have come from his confidence in Arnold's complete trust in him and from his own self-confidence. Arnold was ambitious on Spaatz's behalf and consistently promoted Spaatz's interests during the war. Indeed Arnold was ambitious—and there is full evidence to this effect—that Spaatz should achieve a level of command and recognition equal to that of Eisenhower, and Arnold even sent a letter, "personal eyes only," to Spaatz on this subject via Lovett on one of Lovett's trips to the European theater in 1944. While the ultimate goal that Arnold had in mind was to elevate the role and status of the air arm, Spaatz was his chosen instrument for the purpose.

Spaatz subscribed to the broader purpose but sought no personal recognition. He didn't have to; it was accorded him on merit.

Bradley: I perhaps could talk a little about the West Point part of the picture, which wasn't very illuminating on General Spaatz. I had experiences similar to this myself. I had five roommates while I was at the Academy. One died before we graduated, one was turned back to another class because of academics, and there were three others—Fred Castle, Orin Haugen, and Bob Wood. Fred Castle was killed leading a wing for LeMay in England during the last part of the war and received the Medal of Honor posthumously. Bob Wood became a four-star general in the Army. And Orin Haugen was sort of a Spaatz; he just didn't have a chance to work at it long enough. Orin was a complete, absolute failure as a cadet. He never wore a stripe. He, too, was walking the area the last week of the four years, and as far as I know, he didn't care. He graduated much lower in his class than General Spaatz. After graduation Orin Haugen became one of the finest young officers in the cavalry, and he was killed as a commander of a paratrooper regiment attacking Manila. So you can see, Orin would probably have gone a long way just like General Spaatz.

Holley: I would like to take up a small point about the time just before World War II when General Spaatz was assigned to command the Materiel Division at Wright Field in Ohio. There is a nice account in an oral history interview with Gen. Orval Cook about Cook taking a rather complicated technical problem to Spaatz soon after his arrival.* Spaatz was appalled at the complexity of the problem and he thereupon decided, "This is not for me; I am simply not up to handling this job." He had self-confidence (as you have just pointed out, Al), enormous confidence in himself as a tactical unit commander, but he realized that his engineering background was not up to it so he pulled out. I can't vouch for the truth of this; I am only reporting what Orval Cook said. Obviously Orval Cook was a man of very real technical capability, as we all know from his work, for example, as the chief of the propeller section in the early days out at Wright Field.

What occurs to me is that Spaatz had that quality of objectivity, which you mentioned. The most important sense of objectivity is to be able to see oneself as one really is and to recognize one's limitations. It is a pretty difficult thing to back away from an assignment. The normal, gung-ho

---

*In 1939 Capt. Orval Cook (1898–1980) joined the engineering section at Wright Field; he had served in the aircraft branch there during the early 1930s. He received his fourth star in 1954 when he was Deputy Commander in Chief, European Command. See intvw, Hugh N. Ahman and Maj Richard Emmons, USAF Oral History Program, with Gen Cook, Jun 4–5 and Aug 6–7, 1974, USAF Historical Research Center, Maxwell AFB, Alabama, K239.0512-740, pp 294–95.

AIR LEADERSHIP

answer is to salute and say "yes sir" and carry on even if you don't have the capabilities. I think that is a very impressive attribute: that he realized he was into something for which he was not really geared. I am only taking Orval Cook's word on this, but it has a ring of authenticity in the details. It is quite extensively treated in Cook's oral history.

Mets: That is perfectly in character, I think. During General Spaatz's briefings to Secretary Stimson and General Marshall before he took the Eighth Air Force overseas, he repeatedly made the point (I think he was doing it for General Arnold) that we didn't want to get premature about this, we didn't want to build up a publicity campaign that would cause us to commit our forces to battle before they were ready—because a failure would be so costly to the Air Force that we would never be able to show our stuff over Germany. It may have been one of the lessons he learned during the airmail crisis, because General Foulois was rather too ready to take on anything.* At that time (although not very much noticed in the literature on the airmail crisis) Spaatz was working directly for General Westover,[†] just one level below General Foulois. The way that Foulois suffered because of the apparent failure of the Army in airmail must have been an important lesson to General Spaatz that would make him urge caution on Hap Arnold many times afterwards.

LeMay: I think I am a little skeptical about that. I can't imagine General Spaatz dodging any job. Remember before the war we didn't have an air force. We had three groups in the United States and some provisional groups—one in Panama, one in Hawaii, and one in the Philippines. So no one got any great amount of command experience. I guess General Spaatz had commanded a group once. I personally never commanded anything. I did have a squadron when we started to expand. I was a squadron commander for ten days. I had no airplanes, no equipment, and about twenty percent of the people I was supposed to have. That was my command experience. I never felt that I was qualified to take over any job I was assigned starting with the war. I think most everybody felt the same way, but they had to do it. So you dug in and did the best you could.

Gunderson: What did you look for in selecting a good commander?

---

*Maj. Gen. Benjamin D. Foulois (1879–1967) was Chief of the Army Air Corps 1931–35. A Senate investigation of improprieties in granting airmail contracts prompted President Franklin D. Roosevelt to cancel those contracts in February 1934 and have the Air Corps take over the job. Severe winter weather soon exposed the inadequacy of Air Corps equipment and training—costing the lives of twelve pilots. See John F. Shiner, *Foulois and the U.S. Army Air Corps, 1931–1935* (Washington, 1983).

[†]Brig. Gen. Oscar Westover (1883–1938) was Assistant to the Chief of Air Corps, Maj. Gen. Foulois, whom Westover replaced in 1935. Maj. Gen. Westover's tour as Chief was ended by a fatal aircraft accident.

LeMay: The trait that I thought was most valuable was a sense of responsibility. I would forgive a mistake if somebody did something in a crisis and did the wrong thing, but I couldn't forgive the guy that sat there and did nothing. He had to realize that when he was in command, he was responsible not only for his people but for the mission and everything else; everything was on his shoulders, and he had to accept that. That's the thing that I demanded in my people more than anything else. One mistake he could make. I didn't want anybody making a lot of mistakes. I couldn't take time to train the slow learners; that's what it amounted to. Responsibility is the main thing that I demanded.

Bradley: I think Curt pretty well put it the way I feel about it. Of course, in my business, you had to look for some technical expertise too. In general, as Curt has put it, you have got to take the guy that will take the responsibility and get in there and pitch.

Gunderson: No one has commented on it today, but somewhere along the line, there are situations where you have to be willing to take a chance—the calculated risk.

LeMay: I just thought of something that might have influenced General Spaatz in running down this technical job. Remember, Mark, up at Selfridge Field when we took the examination to go to the engineering school at Wright Field?

Bradley: I didn't take an exam there, but I went to the engineering school.

LeMay: I did. Maybe it was before you got up there. They gave an exam up through calculus to see whether you qualified to go down to this august establishment. I took the exam, and then when I got back from overseas duty and went to Langley Field, we were in and out of Wright Field quite frequently getting the latest navigation equipment and working with the B–17s on long-range flights and so forth. I was over there one day, and I wanted to get something done about the maps. The only aeronautical charts we had then were Rand-McNally maps and naval hydrographic charts; there was no place to keep them in the B–17. I wanted a place to keep the maps.

Somebody said, "What do you want?" I said, "Get some stovepipe and roll up the maps and stick them in the stovepipe." They went off and called somebody, and in half an hour, a gentleman came up in a long white coat and a black bow tie—the superintendent of the sheet metal shop. I told him what I wanted, and he said, "How do you want them fastened together?" We said, "Any way; get a board and drill a hole in it and stick them down in that." I had to call the carpenter shop, and another gentleman came up with a white coat and a black bow tie, and I told him what we wanted. It took us all day to get four pieces of stovepipe set in a couple of boards to lean up against the wall in a B–17. I didn't think much of that.

AIR LEADERSHIP

I went over to the personnel office at Wright Field and said, "Am I still on the list to be ordered out here?" They got the big ledger out. I took a pencil and scratched a line through my name and closed the book and gave it back to them, and I haven't heard anything from Wright Field since. Maybe Tooey felt something like that.

Goldberg: I don't think Spaatz would have made it in any other branch of the service than the Air Corps. He was too unorthodox, too irreverent, too much of an individualist. My guess is that had he been assigned to another branch and had to spend any time in it after World War I, he would have left the service. As it was he almost left the Air Service anyway at one point in the 1920s. I am certain that he could not have lasted in the Infantry, either on his own initiative or that of his superiors.

Mets: The division of labor in World War II was extremely fortunate. In World War II you had Arnold in Washington doing a vital job that I am pretty sure Spaatz could not have done. I don't think Arnold would have been nearly as good as Spaatz in Europe. In part by accident or pure fortune, you had the man, I think, absolutely best qualified for combat command over in Europe, and Air Staff leadership, which is an entirely different thing, was done very adeptly by General Arnold. They were not interchangeable officers by any means. I don't think Spaatz would have made it in Washington during wartime.

Question: Russell Weigley's *Eisenhower's Lieutenants* mentions the enormous compassion and concern that Spaatz had for his airmen.* Would you comment on that?

LeMay: I think it is important, but you can carry it too far. I have known commanders who were complete failures because they worried too much about their people. Maybe that is phrasing it badly. They let their worry about casualties influence their decisions, and they probably wound up by not getting the job done and losing more people doing it poorly than they would have done otherwise. I have also known some people who went completely to pieces because they couldn't stand the casualties. It is something that I always worried about. After every mission I always wondered could I have done something else or should I have done it in another way that might have saved some airplanes and people. Usually I couldn't think of anything, but it is something you always think about, something you always should think about. You can't fight a war without losing some people. The best you can do is do the best you can to accomplish your mission with the lowest possible losses. If you don't think about that, I think you are a poor commander.

---

*Russell F. Weigley, *Eisenhower's Lieutenants: The Campaign of France and Germany, 1944–1945* (Bloomington, Ind., 1981).

MODELS

Mets: Every commander has got to balance the need to get the mission done with compassion for his troops. General Spaatz was a very, very taciturn person, and he didn't wear this kind of emotion on his sleeve. He had been brought up in the era of aviation where you were losing friends every Monday and Wednesday. Our accident rate since World War II has gone down dramatically. Mrs. Spaatz was telling me just yesterday about his schoolmate from West Point who later on was his number two at Issoudun in France. Before his eyes Major Benedict crashed into a balloon at Langley Field in 1925 and was killed. That apparently caused Spaatz to get considerably upset. It certainly caused Mrs. Spaatz to get upset. Later on it fell to Spaatz, during World War II, to write to the widow again because Benedict's son was killed in a B–24 accident out in the Pacific during the war. Another of Spaatz's close friends was Clarence Tinker, and Spaatz also had to write that widow twice—once for the father and once for the son.

Where the story of Spaatz's compassion culminates for me is after the war. I can quote this directly from an interview with Secretary Symington.* An American C–47 was shot down by the Yugoslavians in the summer of 1946. Naturally Secretary Symington and General Spaatz went over to Arlington for the funeral. The widow was there, and she was crying. Secretary Symington confesses that he himself was crying, and General Spaatz stood up like an iron soldier. When they got back to the Pentagon, Symington, feeling weak at having broken down, said to Spaatz, "My you are a cool bastard." General Spaatz, who never was very emotional in either his oral communications or his written communications, turned snow white, then beet red, and said, "Goddamn you, my life has been nothing but one long attendance at the funerals of my friends." He turned on his heel and walked to his office.

Holley: It seems to me that General LeMay's point is extremely well taken. If a man is so compassionate that he weakens and can't do the job, obviously he is not going to be an able commander. On the other hand, in the political dimension, it may be very important. Forrest Pogue makes the interesting point in his biography of General Marshall that Marshall would send the weekly casualty figures to Roosevelt and deliberately shove them under his nose, so that he would never forget that every one of those victories cost lives. It seems to me that sheds a lot of light on the character and leadership qualities of Marshall. He wasn't a weakling, obviously, but he never wanted the political leaders to forget that these victories were exceedingly costly.

Goldberg: One form that Spaatz's compassion took was to be honest with his

---

*Stuart Symington (1901–) was Assistant Secretary of War for Air, 1946–47, and the first Secretary of the Air Force, 1947–50.

AIR LEADERSHIP

subordinates and particularly with the combat crews. On one or more occasions during the war, he insisted that they not be misled, that they not be snowed about casualties and their chances and what was happening and what might happen to them. He had to put his foot down on one or more occasions to make certain that they were told the truth. He insisted that they be told the truth. This, it seems to me, was another measure of his objectivity and in a sense his compassion. He was not going to mislead those people, and he didn't.

Question: You implied that General Spaatz probably would not succeed in today's military. What kind of comment is that for today's leadership, but more importantly for the leadership of tomorrow?

Bradley: I don't think I would agree to that. I think he would succeed. I didn't know him very well, but I was on a board with him—the first board in 1939 when we bought the first 500 and some P–40s. He seemed like just as good a man then as anybody else I have ever seen for making decisions and doing things.

Mets: I have mixed emotions about the question. If you look at the class of 1914 from West Point, time and place mean a lot. The 107 members of the class of 1914 were only a little less successful than the class the stars fell on, Ike's class; 26 made general. I happened to look up the figures for the class of 1953 from West Point just recently, and there were 130 who came from that class into the Air Force. Of the 130, only 4 made general. So the difference is very striking. If you are graduating in 1914 and 3 years after graduation you are a major in command of a large training organization and then through a quirk of the regulations you are one of the few from your class who hang onto that majority through the 1920s while most of your classmates are captains, it automatically means you are going to wind up with the command jobs and you are going to wind up with the high staff jobs on General Patrick's staff. To survive that 20 years and go into World War II at the senior field grade level, lieutenant colonel, and benefit from yet another wartime hump—all that was important.

I hope in reading Spaatz's biography, that the young officers of the Air Force will not be seeking concrete laws which will guarantee success with their day-to-day problems in the shop or on the line or wherever—that what they are seeking is to broaden their perspectives, to add vicarious experience, all the time understanding there is no easy answer.

One of the things that I liked about Spaatz was evident when Arnold started hacking on him right after the Battle of the Bulge. It was typical Arnold impatience: "We have got to find a way. We have got to find a strategy to end this thing right now. It is way overdue. How about this renewed Clarion rail plan for all over Germany on one big grand slam?'* Spaatz wrote back, in effect, "Hey, you are getting carried away with these wild ideas. There is no easy, painless panacea." So to some extent he agreed with the British commander, "Bomber" Harris, in that connection. My point here is that I think most historians would say there is no easy model; there are no ironclad laws that are going to come from a reading of history—just a broadening of your experience, a broadening of your perspective.

As for the other part of the question, I admire General Spaatz's approach. It was a pragmatic approach. He would weigh the objectives sought against the cost paid. He was a flexible man who, I think, could change according to the situation. That kind of flexibility, the absence of dogma, makes me hope that he could succeed even in today's Air Force. He did seem to have an aversion for education though, and school is important in today's Air Force.

Goldberg: What has emerged from this discussion about Spaatz was that he was not a model for officers either in his own time or today. This doesn't have a great deal to do with whether he would have succeeded in today's Air Force in becoming a general. What it does say is that in his own time, in spite of being the man that he was, different from most of the other people in the Air Corps in many ways, he was successful. Many others were unsuccessful. A lot of the other people who were his contemporaries during those days would not make it in the modern Air Force either. We are talking about a different time and different generations, and the rules do not apply necessarily from one to the next. I think it very difficult to extrapolate from this discussion anything by way of a model of success, something that today's officers could follow that could help them. We have talked about traits. They are reasonably obvious. We all know about them. Spaatz had good ones; he had some that people didn't consider very good. But once again, to get back to the point I was trying to make, he was unique. I don't think there are any other officers like him—I haven't encountered any—who reached the same level that he did.

Question: I wonder if scale may not have something to do with the successes of people like Spaatz, Arnold, and Brereton? The expansion of the Army Air Forces in World War II created such massive command opportunities relative to a very small number, proportionately, of officers. I'm used to working with the German Army with its large number of officers, and the thing I noticed about both the U.S. Army and Army Air Corps in the

---

*The Clarion plan called for most bombers and fighters of the Eighth, Ninth, and Fifteenth Air Forces to hit hundreds of transportation targets in German villages never before bombed. The plan was tried on February 22 and 23, 1945, but its effect on German transportation and morale was not sufficiently obvious to sustain this tactic.

AIR LEADERSHIP

interwar period is what a small family this was. Marshall had his little black book, and everybody sort of knew everybody else and could sound everybody out. With the tremendous permanent expansion after 1945, those kinds of personal contacts became either less feasible, or they tended to evolve into a sponsorship pattern, which has its own negative side.

Goldberg: I think there is every reason to agree with what you are saying with the exception that the same thing was true of the German Army, which was even smaller, wasn't it, during the same time? Of course, there was no Luftwaffe to speak of before 1934.

It was true in the U.S. Army and to a somewhat lesser extent in the Navy that people did get thrown up to high command very quickly from relatively low ranks. You had instances of officers going from first lieutenant to major general in two or three years. General Eisenhower himself went from colonel to five-star general in a little bit more than three years. So this is inevitable when services are expanded as much as these were. The Army Air Corps expanded something on the order of about one hundred times from 1939 to 1944 when it reached its peak. So it is true that the element of chance was somewhat reduced.

The people who were in charge at the beginning of the war were the most experienced. They had been around the longest time; they were the obvious commanders. Probably our military services expanded more than any others during the course of World War II, because we started from such a small base. The German Army and the Luftwaffe, too, for that matter, had reached a pretty substantial size by the time they launched the war in 1939. We still had an Air Corps of 25,000 in 1939 and an Army of perhaps 165,000.

LeMay: I think that is true, that there was such a small group of people involved here that everyone knew everyone else. The figure I remember is that before the war we had about 1200 officers in the Army Air Corps on active duty—that is, regular officers and reserve officers on active duty—and about 10,000 men. We had some 2,500,000 in the Air Force at the end of the war. So it was a pretty rapid expansion. It is not strange that General Arnold, General Spaatz, General Eaker, and a few others who had the command experience before the war rose to high rank. With the small number of stations we had, there were just a few command slots. If you think you have budget problems now—in 1929–30 there wasn't any travel money to send people around from pillar to post. There was very little command experience in the Army Air Corps, and they had to take advantage of what there was. That doesn't mean that each one of those men succeeded in combat—far from true.

Question: Hiram Bingham in his *An Explorer in the Air Service* took a backhanded slap at Major Spaatz's ability to command and organize the 3d

MODELS

Aviation Instruction Center at Issoudun, France, during World War I.* What was Spaatz's reaction to that?

Mets: Hiram Bingham, as you know, wound up as a U.S. senator. He had some renown in a scientific field, geography perhaps, up at Yale before he came into the service. Spaatz was very, very careful about ever putting anything negative down about another person on paper. I remember just a vague negative reference about one of his schoolmates, Herb Dargue, and another very vague reference about Hiram Bingham's coming along and taking credit for "what we had done at Issoudun."

General Holley has already complained that I have the common biographer's tendency to fall back into a defensive crouch whenever my hero is criticized, and in this case I think I would defend him against Bingham because Bingham got to Issoudun in May 1918. Spaatz got to Issoudun in November 1917 in the company of a man three or four years his senior at West Point, "Mike" Kilner. Kilner was born just four or five years too soon, because (from everything I have read about him) had he been Spaatz's age, Kilner too would have risen to the top. For a while Kilner was the commander at Issoudun and Spaatz was the director of training. When Kilner was promoted to Air Service headquarters, Spaatz remained in command for five months until Bingham took over in August 1918. Kilner and Spaatz built up Issoudun so that before Bingham ever got there, it already had a thousand men, there were furnaces in the barracks, the streets were finished, and they were getting something of a grip on the accident rate.

There are a couple of negative remarks in Bingham's book to the effect that Spaatz cracked up a couple of airplanes—another thing that is not supposed to be a part of our model. That's not good for our survival. I have found records of Spaatz cracking up an airplane in 1931 and records of his losing an airplane landing in "No Man's Land" during World War I. In many ways the records I have from that war are better than those from World War II. I find no other mention of any accidents, so that rather makes me think there was a bad relationship between Bingham and Spaatz. Bingham came along and grabbed the credit for "what we had done," meaning Kilner and Spaatz.

In general, though, Spaatz was not "old West Point." He doesn't fit any pattern of isolation of the military community from civilian society in the years before the war, because even before World War II, I guess, half of Spaatz's friends were civilians. After World War II he moved in civilian circles, among journalists. They were his best friends in the post-retirement years. So I don't think this was an isolated military versus civilian society

---

*Hiram Bingham, *An Explorer in the Air Service* (New Haven, 1920).

kind of thing. It is impossible to reconstruct it at this late date completely, but I instinctively go into the defensive crouch on that particular point.

Goldberg: In World War I, no matter what the air force, any pilot who didn't crack up one or more times just didn't do much flying.

Question: Do you think it is fair to say that Spaatz was a relatively late convert to the escort fighter?

Mets: General Holley and I have corresponded about his article in the *Air University Review* laying part of the blame for the escort thing on my hero.* Spaatz's view was typical for the Air Corps in the 1930s. Most didn't think it was technically feasible to build an escort fighter with sufficient range to accompany the bombers and enough performance to compete with the short-range interceptors that would be sent against them. Spaatz went to England during May 1940 to observe the Battle of Britain. While he was there, he received confirmation of the general notion that the long-range escort fighter was not feasible because the Me–110 was a dismal failure in the Battle of Britain.

So that's an image that he carried back to the Air Staff when he returned in September 1940. For the next two years he continued with this negative idea on the technical feasibility of the long-range fighter. But he didn't reject it wholly. When forming Eighth Air Force here at Bolling Field, both bomber and fighter units were included. Once in England, one of the main things Spaatz did in June and July 1942 was to keep those American fighters from falling into the hands of the British Fighter Command. What he was insisting to the Brits was that these were not defensive weapons, that they were to go as far as they could with the bombers. These fighters were bomber support weapons, rather than air defense weapons. So the mere fact that he brought fighters over and insisted on an offensive role indicated that he thought there might be a requirement for escort fighters.

As General Holley has pointed out, Spaatz's signature is on a document that turned down drop tanks in the spring of 1941. Then he had no knowledge that Hitler would make the bad mistake of invading Russia. If Hitler hadn't invaded Russia, it would have been a whole different ballgame. Enough Me–262s might have been used in time to give the P–51s a strong challenge.

Spaatz had a more or less typical Air Corps attitude on escorts. If there were bad decisions made on the escort thing, he participated in them. He was much less doctrinaire about Air Corps theory than were some other officers,

---

*I. B. Holley, Jr., "Of Saber Charges, Escort Fighters, and Spacecraft," *Air University Review* XXIV, 6 (Sep-Oct 1983), 2–11. Professor Holley discusses the escort issue at greater length in the paper published in this volume.

and that's why Eisenhower wanted him to come back from Africa to take over in England. But if there is blame to be given, Spaatz deserves a part of it.

LeMay: It's not so that General Spaatz found out late that we needed escort fighters. As a matter of fact, one of the things that frustrates me in reading some of the stuff that you people produce is your view of the shortcomings of the Army Air Corps early in the war—for instance, that we couldn't fly without fighter escort. We could fly without fighter escort. I flew clear across Germany one day without fighter escort. It cost me 25 airplanes out of the 125 I had, but we went across, and we got the target. So you could fly without escort, if you were willing to pay the price. But it has always been Air Force doctrine that bombers would be escorted by fighters. Not only that, prior to the war there was doctrine that we would have attack airplanes along to suppress antiaircraft fire. We never did get those, but we got the fighters. We got bombers over there first, because bombers could fly over there. Fighters had to go over by boat, and it took them a little longer.

Then we did misuse them, in my opinion. In the early days the fighter commander thought the best way to protect the bombers was with fighter sweeps out ahead of them. Consequently, they got up as high as they could get, went ahead of us, and never saw any fighters. We went in at a lower altitude, and we saw plenty of them. It wasn't until we got a new fighter commander that we got them down. Then we had fighter support where we could get it right from the start. First, the RAF Spitfires were sent along, and they wouldn't go very far. Then we got the P-47s; they went with us, when we finally got them to fly with us, as far as they could go. We were always demanding more and more range for the fighters, because we knew the price was going to be heavy if we had to penetrate without them.

We didn't need the attack airplanes, because we found out that the flak wasn't the big problem we thought it was going to be. Airplanes were shot down, yes, but we completely ignored flak on all the missions in Europe, and certainly I did over in the Marianas. It was there, and something I had to contend with, but we ignored it. We picked the best route for approach to the target for considerations other than flak and went right through it. They used to take evasive action, but I started out by not taking any at all, and I lost fewer airplanes than those who were zigzagging around trying to dodge the flak. So everybody started doing that and flew through it and ignored it.

General Spaatz wanted the fighters as much as anyone else. They weren't available; when he got them, they were used, and they continued to be used right up to the end of the war. And they will probably be used if we can get them to fly far enough in any future wars. You will have a combined attack.

II. PORTRAITS

Gen. Ira C. Eaker
1896–

In a two-volume history of early Army air leadership, DeWitt Copp has provided especially detailed portraits of Frank Andrews, Hap Arnold, Tooey Spaatz, and Ira Eaker. Of the four, only Eaker was still alive when Copp set to work. So fully did Eaker give of his time and memory that Copp dedicated the second volume to him: "One of the first and one of the few." Among Eaker's warmest memories were those of Marshal of the RAF Sir Arthur "Bomber" Harris, who took over RAF Bomber Command two days after Eaker reached England in 1942 to build Eighth Air Force Bomber Command. The Chief of the Air Historical Branch in the Ministry of Defence, Air Commodore Henry Probert, RAF, Retired, recalls that friendship and the Anglo-American alliance which proved so formidable during World War II.—W.T.

DeWitt Copp's Portrait of American Air Leadership

Henry A. Probert

It is a great privilege to have been invited to give the address on this very special occasion. As one who joined the Royal Air Force in 1948 and has been committed to it ever since, I belong to that generation who have regarded the bonds between our two air forces as an article of faith. I think they are closer than those between the sister services in our two countries, and indeed I believe they are probably unique in history. I therefore know that this evening I am among friends.

I have been asked to comment from the British angle on Pete Copp's two fascinating volumes* —and I must try to avoid the many pitfalls that inevitably confront any Brit who holds forth on this side of the Atlantic. I am reminded of a story related by Marshal of the RAF Sir John Slessor,[†] who contributed perhaps more than anyone else to establishing the ties between us. A British officer on a trip to Washington visited many of the sights and came to Lafayette Square. "Why do you call it the White House?" "We painted it white when it was done up after you Brits burned Washington in 1812." "You don't mean to tell me we burnt Washington?" "Didn't you know you goddamn Limeys burned Washington in 1812?" "I'm most terribly sorry—I had no idea—Joan of Arc yes, but I thought Washington died a natural death."

So I must be careful. Moreover, since I have not yet had the opportunity to carry out a major piece of historical writing myself, I am bound to approach someone like Pete Copp with considerable humility. Works such as his do not materialise out of thin air, and these clearly represent much diligent research, consultation, and sheer hard work. I am bound to say, however, that I do not always find the story easy to follow; I would find it

---

*DeWitt S. Copp, *A Few Great Captains: The Men and Events that Shaped the Development of U.S. Air Power* (Garden City, N.Y., 1980) and *Forged in Fire: Strategy and Decisions in the Air War over Europe 1940–45* (Garden City, N.Y., 1982).

[†]Ed. note: Marshal of the RAF Sir John Slessor (1897–1979) was Chief of Air Staff 1950–52. During World War II he participated in Anglo-American staff conversations (1941); served as Assistant Chief of Air Staff for Policy (1942–43); led RAF Coastal Command (1943) and RAF Mediterranean and Middle East (1944–45).

AIR LEADERSHIP

helpful to have the occasional chart showing the organisational pattern and who was doing what at particular times. A few maps would help too. Then again I do not think they are fully enough referenced; all too many statements are made without any indication of the authority for them, and one just has to take them on trust—something one is reluctant to do when one spots the occasional inaccuracy.

I must admit, too, some disappointment that so few reputable British sources are drawn upon or even mentioned. I have no complaint about works such as those by Slessor, Sir Winston Churchill, and R. V. Jones, but one really must be careful of sensationalist authors. To fail to refer to the British official histories and the better memoirs and biographies strikes me as most surprising. I am thinking especially of *The Strategic Air Offensive Against Germany* by Sir Charles Webster and Noble Frankland; Sir Arthur Harris's *Bomber Offensive*; the biographies of Lord Trenchard and Sir Charles Portal by Andrew Boyle and Denis Richards respectively; and H. Montgomery Hyde's *British Air Policy Between the Wars*. On a subject such as this, where the policies of our two air forces were so closely related, I would regard such volumes as prime sources.

Having got that off my chest—without I hope giving offence—let me turn to the story itself, and here let me say straightaway that I found both volumes most informative and learned a very great deal. Clearly in the short time I have this evening I cannot comment in detail, but I am going to reflect on two of the major themes that run through both books and are of particular interest to the British reader.

The first theme is, quite simply, the control of air power, where there is a major contrast between your experience and ours. If we take the years immediately after World War I as our starting point, we both suffered from severely limited military budgets, but we in the U.K. already had our independent Air Force. This resulted essentially from the scale of air operations that had built up over several years of war, plus growing competition between the Army and Navy for the supply of aircraft, engines, etc., and the public outcry over the unopposed German bombing of London, especially by day. This showed how air power could be used independently of land or naval operations and was a major factor influencing the recommendations of Lt. Gen. J. C. Smuts* in 1917:

> The Air Service can be used as an independent means of air operations—nobody who witnessed the attack on London on 7 July could have any doubt on that point. As far as at present can be foreseen there is absolutely no limit to the scale of its future independent war use. And the day may not be far off when aerial operations with

---

*Ed. note: Lt. Gen. (later Field Marshal) Jan Christian Smuts (1870–1950) was South African representative in the Imperial War Cabinet 1917–18.

> their devastation of enemy lands and destruction of industrial and populous centres on a vast scale may become the principal operations of war, to which the older forms of military and naval operations may become secondary and subordinate.[1]

This was indeed one of the most important prophecies ever made about air power, reaching partial fulfillment in World War II and—I suggest—total fulfillment in the deterrent strategy that has prevented all-out conflict ever since 1945. There were those in 1917 who, while not totally opposed like the Navy, still doubted the wisdom of making such a major organisational change in the middle of the war—among them Trenchard* —and it was Smuts' insistence, strongly supported by General Sir David Henderson[+] of the Royal Flying Corps, that ensured the scheme went through. Otherwise there is very little doubt that we, like you, would not have become independent during the interwar years. You got away with this failure, but frankly I doubt very much if we should have done it. It is a strange paradox that while the basic case for our independent RAF rested on a belief in the strategic role of air power, it was in the defensive role that the RAF won its first great victory—and it was its independent status that made that victory possible. I just do not believe that a Royal Flying Corps firmly under Army control would have allowed the unfettered development of the Fighter Command that enabled us to win the Battle of Britain. As Slessor said: "If the RAF had been split up again between the two older Services after the First War, it would have suffered the fate of the Tank Corps and we should have lost the Battle of Britain."[2]

So we in the U.K. have cause to be thankful for the truly inspired decision to create the independent RAF amid the tumult of World War I. Nevertheless I find it totally unsurprising that you did not go the same way. You had been in the war for a much shorter time, your military aviation could not develop on the same scale, and you were far from the scene of the action. Moreover, if I read Pete Copp aright, you had made no attempt to study and draw lessons from the war in Europe prior to April 1917. So at the end of the war yours was a long uphill struggle to win for your air force more and more freedom from Army control, but I find it intriguing that one of our great arguments for maintaining the RAF intact—the indivisibility of air power—never seems to have been used. Throughout your campaign for independence the right of the U.S. Navy to run its own aviation was never

---

*Ed. note: Maj. Gen. (later Marshal of the RAF) Hugh Trenchard (1873–1956) commanded the Royal Flying Corps in the Field 1915–17. When in the last year of World War I the Royal Flying Corps and the Royal Naval Air Service joined to form the Royal Air Force, Trenchard became the first Chief of Air Staff—a positon he held again for a decade after that war.

[+]Ed. note: Lt. Gen. Sir David Henderson (1862–1921) commanded the Royal Flying Corps 1915–17.

AIR LEADERSHIP

challenged, and indeed there was obviously enormous growth of naval aviation throughout the interwar years—presumably with competition for resources and little if any coordination of design, procurement, training, tactical doctrine, and so on. It is a major subject, of course, and I would not have expected detailed coverage, but I would have found it helpful to hear from Pete Copp a little more about the growth of naval flying so as to give a better perspective—though he does provide a brief but illuminating summary of naval attitudes early in the second volume. For you then, the debate with the Navy was limited to deciding where to draw the dividing line: your shipborne aircraft automatically belonged to the Navy, and it was only the land-based maritime aircraft that one argued about—as for example, in 1941, when your Navy intended to operate land-based bombers.

For us, on the other hand, there was a unity about air power and the profession of flying. I recall Slessor criticising your Adm. Ernest King's* view that the basic profession of the maritime airman was sailing; in Slessor's judgement the profession was that of an airman, regardless of where he flew. Consequently, while you were fighting between the wars for the independence of land-based air power, we were struggling to *retain* the independence of *all forms* of air power. It was a fight we did not entirely win, for in 1937 the Navy regained control of its shipborne aircraft, the Fleet Air Arm, but by that time the continued independence of the rest of the RAF was assured. Our debate with the Navy has of course gone on, with repeated bids from them for the transfer of land-based maritime aircraft, including one at a critical time in late 1940—though I don't think our Navy ever went so far as to insist that the RAF should not operate more than a hundred miles offshore, as Pete Copp says yours insisted. Indeed one can detect continued rumblings of the controversy in our recent Falklands operations, but here I am straying beyond my brief.

I suppose it does not really surprise me that, in your circumstances in North America, military aviation was allowed to develop for so long as an appendage of the two older services. One could hardly expect the Morrow Board in 1925 to ignore the basic tenet of American foreign policy, namely isolationism; if your armed forces were maintained only for home defence there was no role for strategic air power and therefore no real case for an independent air force—bearing in mind the available technology. In our case in Europe, with operating ranges far shorter, the independent role was practicable much earlier, but for you over here, given the political determination not to get involved in other peoples' wars and given the state of the

---

*Ed. note: Fleet Adm. Ernest J. King (1878–1956) was Chief of Naval Operations 1942–45.

PORTRAITS

aviation art, the proponents of an independent air force could really have little going for them. I do wonder, however, if when men such as Arnold were putting forward their ideas for greater independence, they had in mind or indeed used in argument our practice in Great Britain; in fact I read with amazement Pete Copp's statement that Benny Foulois was refused permission to use in evidence the practice of other countries.

I am astonished, too, that at the beginning of World War II, Arnold was not privileged to sit on the Joint Army-Navy Board where military strategy was worked out, whereas in our situation the Chief of the Air Staff was on a par with his opposite numbers for all purposes and could exercise enormous influence in times of crisis. One has only to think, for example, of the Battle of France, when Cyril Newall* and Hugh Dowding† fought successfully to prevent Fighter Command being whittled away. Fortunately for you, once the Army Air Forces were created, Arnold was at last given enhanced status, and I would agree that independence would have been wrong at that time with expansion so urgent; Slessor, who claims to have been consulted in 1941 while in the U.S.A. on the desirability of setting up an autonomous air force, advised against it since he thought there were too few experienced officers to run it.

So you ended up fighting your war under the umbrella of the Army. But in case you are tempted to think we had no such problems, I would remind you that there were occasions when the British Army was so dissatisfied with the extent to which the RAF could meet its needs that it asked for its supporting air forces to be organised within it. In late 1939, for example, Trenchard was writing to Lord Swinton‡ seeking support in the face of alleged Army pressure for its own air force, and in 1942 Portal§ had to point out that such a scheme would effectively mean the division of the RAF into three separate services and extinguish all hope of developing the bomber offensive; the issue as he defined it was whether we continued to maintain a centralised and flexible force or destroyed the cohesion of our growing air power. What this really comes down to is the fact that there will *never* be enough aircraft to satisfy all who want them, and it is all too easy for those

---

*Ed. note: Air Chief Marshal (later Marshal of the RAF) Sir Cyril Newall (1886–1963) was Chief of Air Staff 1937–40.

†Ed. note: Air Chief Marshal Sir Hugh Dowding (1882–1970) led Fighter Command 1936–40.

‡Ed. note: Philip Cunliffe-Lister, Viscount Swinton (1884–1972) was Secretary of State for Air 1935–38.

§Ed. note: Marshal of the RAF Sir Charles Portal (1893–1971) was Chief of Air Staff 1940–45.

AIR LEADERSHIP

who feel they have not got their fair share to seek the answer in changing the organisation.

So much then for the control of air power. Now for the second theme, its use as a strategic weapon independently of naval and land forces—and I hope you will not mind my starting by reminding you again of that prophesy by Smuts in 1917 about the potential of strategic bombing. The independent force we then created in France had little time to achieve anything. Indeed one wonders what would have happened to it had the war gone on into 1919 and what the consequences would have been for the development of strategic bombing doctrine. As it was, we went into the peacetime years assuming, largely on the basis of our experience in the German attacks on London, that strategic bombing was bound to be a highly potent weapon in any future war, and our Home Defence Air Force was constituted on the premise that the best form of defence would be offence. In other words, the strategic bombing force, which Baldwin said would always get through, was there to assist in defending the country by posing a threat to the enemy. It was thus a primitive form of deterrence. Over here you had that small group of aviators who believed passionately that strategic bombing was the weapon of the future but were unable to convince either the main military establishment or the politicians; as Pete Copp clearly explains, they were simply ahead of their time. Nevertheless, I find it thought-provoking that, whereas we did not even issue the first specifications for our four-engined bombers until 1936, your first B–17 arrived at Langley Field the following year, fully three years before our first Stirling appeared.

The distressing aspect of this is that, given your early lead, you were not allowed to exploit it. When the European War started, particularly after the fall of France, your politicians seemed more eager to export military aircraft to us than to equip their own Air Corps. For us, of course, the assistance we received in this way was of incalculable value, and the generosity of the decision in 1940 to split your aircraft production equally with us needs no underlining by me. Yet I cannot but sympathise with Arnold's dilemma. Believing that the U.S.A. needed an air force in being, he was really facing the greatest problem that ever confronts the military commander: where is the decisive point? Just as we in the U.K. had to insist in 1940 that the Battle of France was not the crucial point and that our fighter force must be kept intact for the decisive battle that was still to come, you had to weigh the merits of sending desperately needed equipment across the Atlantic, knowing that if we nevertheless were to collapse you would be putting your own position in jeopardy. You took the risk, for which we must be eternally grateful, but I find it easy to understand the anxieties that Arnold felt and which Pete Copp clearly brings out.

PORTRAITS

This brings me now to the years in which your air force and ours came to work together in a really quite remarkable way; indeed as I read *Forged in Fire* it seemed that that title could be applied not only to the power and position the U.S. Army Air Forces itself achieved in the heat of battle, but equally to the bonds that were formed between the USAAF and the RAF through that same process. These bonds were marked in part by the close friendships that were quickly established between your senior airmen and ours. Pete Copp rightly draws attention to some of these. For example, when Spaatz visited us in the dark days of 1940 in what must be seen as the beginning of the special relationship between our two air forces, he formed a particular liking for and respect for Slessor who was to exercise enormous influence on RAF policy over the next ten to fifteen years. Slessor in turn was greatly encouraged when Spaatz told him that he believed Fighter Command would win the Battle of Britain and that without air superiority the Germans would not invade.

Then in 1941, as Pete Copp reminds us, Arnold came over and witnessed the German bombing at first hand. Slessor, who had first met Arnold in Washington in 1940 and saw much of him in later years, had great affection and respect for him:

> He was an intensely likeable person, transparently honest, terrifically energetic, given to unorthodox methods and, though shrewd and without many illusions, always with something of a schoolboy naivete about him. One of the earliest Air Officers in the United States Army, he had lived through years of frustration which had done nothing to impair his effervescent enthusiasm or his burning faith in the future of air power. He wore himself out in the service of his country.[3]

Arnold's opposite number, of course, was Portal, and his biographer quotes him as saying in later years:

> I have always regarded General Arnold as a wonderful co-operator, a great helper at the beginning of your participation in the war in helping the RAF to get the aircraft we so badly needed from America. And another thing I remember very clearly is his intense keenness to benefit from our experience. He was absolutely without preconceived ideas—he appeared to have only one object, which was to get the right answer to all of his problems.[4]

It was shortly after Pearl Harbor, when Portal was here in Washington and saw some antiaircraft guns in position, that he offered to give Arnold a dollar for every bomb that fell on Washington during the war; if none fell, Arnold was to give him ten dollars at the end of the war. Arnold duly paid up. His letter reads as follows:

> I am very glad to send you superimposed herewith the 10 bucks that I owe you. Glad in that we here in U.S. did not get the punishment that came with aerial bombing. But who knows? Aerial bombing might have perhaps added impetus to our efforts—ended the war sooner—saved many lives.[5]

Then again there was the close friendship between Eaker and Harris. While they differed on how to carry out strategic bombing, there was—as

AIR LEADERSHIP

Pete Copp reminds us—no personal animosity whatsoever. Here I can do no better than remind you of what Harris himself wrote:

> If I were asked what were the relations between Bomber Command and the American Bomber Force I would say that we had no relations. The word is inapplicable to what actually happened; we and they were one force. The Americans gave us the best they had, and they gave us everything we needed as and when the need arose. I hope, indeed, I know, that we did everything possible for them in return. We could have had not better brothers in arms than Ira Eaker, Fred Anderson and Jimmy Doolittle, and the Americans could have had no better commanders than these three. I was, and am, privileged to count all three of them as the closest of friends. As for the American bomber crews, they were the bravest of the brave, and I know that I am speaking for my own bomber crews when I pay this tribute.[6]

I did not know when I prepared my address for tonight that by the time I came to deliver these words Sir Arthur would be dead. I am sure many of you here remember him and all he did for the Anglo-American Alliance and share our feelings at this time. May I leave you with just one little test question that he used to try on his visitors: "When did the first aerial reconnaissance take place?" The obvious response would be something like balloons in 1870. Then he would smile: "It's in the Bible, where it says that Noah first sent forth the raven and then the dove!"

While on the subject of commanders, I must mention Eaker's most moving appeal to Arnold of March 1943, which Pete Copp quotes at length. Eaker's suggestion that Arnold did not understand the operational realities in Europe was echoed by none other than Portal, who asked Trenchard to tell the senior Air Force officers in the States that many of them knew nothing about European conditions. It was high time, said Portal, that they trusted and supported their commanders in the field—not worry them with theories and ideas conceived three thousand miles from the front. It was in the same sort of spirit that Slessor rounded on Sir Archibald Sinclair,* as Pete Copp says, telling him not to expect the USAAF to overcome all its problems overnight. In other words, what we see in these wartime years is the professional airmen of both air forces coming together to help and encourage each other on all sorts of occasions; it is one of the great lessons in the history of our two nations that we shall forget at our peril.

This is not to say that there were not honest disagreements, and none greater than the different attitudes toward unescorted daylight bombing. Yet in the prewar days your belief that the bomber could defend itself successfully without needing fighter escort was essentially shared by us. What we both reckoned without was the development of radar, making possible an efficient control and reporting system, coupled with fighter aircraft gaining a marked speed advantage over the bomber. As Slessor later admitted, we in the U.K.

---

*Ed. note: Sir Archibald Sinclair (1890–1970) was Secretary of State for Air 1940–45.

underrated the efficacy of fighter defence, and it was in opposition to the views of most of the RAF "establishment" that Sir Thomas Inskip* insisted in 1937 on giving it a higher priority (as Pete Copp rightly reminds us). The surprising thing is that we did not read from this any lessons about the vulnerability of our own bombers to enemy fighter defences—until of course we began to find it out the hard way. Then, having sustained heavy losses in some of our daylight attacks, we decided our strategic bombing could only be done by night. The Germans, too, after the experience of the Battle of Britain—the first time they had met properly organised fighter opposition other than at Dunkirk—had to switch to night attacks.

Yet as Pete Copp makes clear, Spaatz remained firm in his belief in daylight bombing, provided the aircraft had enough defensive firepower. It seems to have been only a few of your leaders who at that stage appreciated the implications of the air fighting in Europe. Since neither you nor we believed a long-range escort fighter could be built, you had to construct your strategic bombing force on the assumption it would be self-defending—unless of course you accepted that your bombing too would have to be done by night. That was not something that the RAF were keen to see happen, though (according to Slessor) Churchill had grave doubts in 1942 about your ability to bomb the German heartland by day without enormous casualties. Slessor himself, however, believed you would be able to do so once you got really adequate numbers, and our Air Staff urged Churchill not to try to divert your air force from the role for which it had been trained.

Portal too gave your policy very strong support, realising that successful precision bombing would be more deadly than area attack, and that round-the-clock bombing would be better than day or night alone; moreover, remembering how long it had taken the RAF to build up its night bombing potential, he and his colleagues were much more patient and understanding of your early problems than were our politicians or your own people back home. Even so, privately Portal had grave doubts whether you could get away with it, and Slessor thought his own influence might have been critical:

> Somehow I was always convinced that they would pull it off. I admit I was only backing a very strong hunch—which one must sometimes do in war. Perhaps it was just as well that I did. Some who have studied the contemporary records far more carefully than I have had an opportunity of doing think it possible that, if I had not taken that line at the time, the American bomber offensive in Europe might have been stillborn.[7]

So what of the bombing campaign itself? Ours of course began in 1940 and from what Pete Copp says both Spaatz and Arnold appreciated its importance, though in 1941 the latter had little regard for what it was

---

*Ed. note: Sir Thomas Inskip (1876–1947) was Minister for the Co-ordination of Defence 1936–39.

AIR LEADERSHIP

achieving; he was of course correct. We were having to learn the business the hard way (as you too had to do later on), and we needed time to develop the right kind of aircraft, improve the navigational aids, train the crews, and so on. Nevertheless we were trying to hit back in the only way possible, something essential for morale both in the U.K. and in the occupied countries, and we were laying the foundations for the future. Overall what Arnold saw reinforced his belief in the potential of strategic bombing. Subsequently, as the likelihood of your becoming involved in the war increased, you based your planning on the assumption that air power could be brought to bear on Germany long before the Army would be able to invade. As John Terraine will remind us most strongly in his forthcoming book about the RAF in World War II, the RAF "stood on the right of the line" for much of the war, and that was true for the USAAF also.[8]

I cannot possibly go into detail on the joint campaign as it developed, but can merely make a few observations. The first is to stress the influence that your entry into the war had on our decision to press on with the bomber offensive. Early 1942 was a critical time, as Pete Copp says; if we drew back, there was every chance your strategy would concentrate on Japan rather than Germany. The policy of "Germany first" could be sustained only if we showed you our determination to back it—which meant strategic bombing. Secondly (and all too many authors miss this point) we had to be seen to be giving active support to the Russians, who were engaging the main body of the main enemy, to use Terraine's phrase. The bomber offensive was the Second Front for which they were clamouring, and Stalin (as Slessor says) attached great importance to it. Despite all the ideas we considered for invading northwestern Europe in 1942, and indeed 1943, there really was no way we were going to make and sustain a successful landing until 1944, so we just *had* to press on with the bombing campaign.

This leads to my third point: it was at precisely this moment in early 1942 that the force had been built up to the level at which it could begin to come good. True, there were many setbacks and we never achieved all that the proponents of strategic bombing hoped we could, but from then on we forced the Germans onto the defensive; of all our achievements—and of course I mean yours combined with ours—perhaps the greatest was the amount of effort we compelled the Germans to devote to the defence of their homeland, thus relieving the pressure on the various land fronts. The fact that the Luftwaffe was eventually unable to support the Wehrmacht on the Eastern Front, in the Mediterranean theatre, and then in the Battle of Normandy, was really quite crucial, and for this the overall strategic bombing campaign must take much of the credit.

My fourth point stems from this. Believing that more effort should have been devoted to the Battle of the Atlantic, the Royal Navy never really reconciled itself to the strategic bomber offensive—and never was its opposition greater than in 1942. Pete Copp rightly observes that Bomber Command was contributing to the maritime war through its attacks on U-boat bases and production, and through mine laying. I am sure we and you were right not to allow the naval lobbies to restrict the buildup of the bombing offensive. Wars are won by attacking the enemy, not by defending against his attacks. But I do think we air historians should remember how critical the Battle of the Atlantic was. After all, our ability to mount the combined bomber offensive depended on our keeping open the Atlantic supply lines. The navies had a point, and we historians need to keep a balanced view.

Finally, could strategic bombing possibly have won the European war? As Pete Copp says, "outside the minds of a few vintage airmen—US and RAF—there were no military or political leaders who believed Hitler could be overcome by air bombardment alone."[9] Certainly, Harris believed it was possible had we built up a large enough force and then concentrated its efforts on the bombing of Germany to the exclusion of all else. Churchill, whose attitude toward bombing was far from consistent, did not think so. Nor did Portal who, despite his firm advocacy of the strategic bombing campaign, came to realise that its main function was to prepare the way for Overlord.

There was of course the controversy between area bombing and what Harris called panacea bombing, with the RAF convinced that area bombing was the only practical means while you believed precision attacks were the way forward. Had we been able to agree on this matter, maybe we should have achieved more, though in the event the two types of bombing complemented each other pretty well and were at times indistinguishable. I think it is arguable that our demand for unconditional surrender merely served to stiffen the enemy's resistance, and that without it the effect of our bombing on German morale might have been greater, but that is merely speculation. Even if Germany had come to terms under our bombing and prior to Overlord, the Eastern Front would still have been perhaps the determining factor. In my view, then, given the state of the art, strategic bombing could not have won the war against Germany on its own, but I very much doubt if we could ever have won without it.

I am very conscious that I have left many important things unsaid, but I hope I have done enough to stimulate your own thoughts and to show that—despite the criticisms I mentioned at the beginning—I believe Pete Copp has put together a fascinating and most valuable account, one which on all the really important aspects of the story has got it right.

Notes

1. Quoted in H. Montgomery Hyde, *British Air Policy Between the Wars, 1918–1939* (London, 1976), p 31.
2. Marshal of the RAF Sir John Slessor, *The Central Blue* (London, 1956), p 46.
3. *Ibid*, p 326.
4. Quoted in Denis Richards, *Portal of Hungerford* (London, 1977), p 214.
5. *Ibid*, p 249.
6. Marshal of the RAF Sir Arthur Harris, *Bomber Offensive* (London, 1947), p 246.
7. Slessor, p 432.
8. John Terraine, *The Right of the Line* (London, 1985). The American title is *A Time for Courage* (New York, 1985); see especially pp 681–87.
9. DeWitt S. Copp, *Forged in Fire: Strategy and Decisions in the Air War over Europe, 1940–1945*, (Garden City, N.Y., 1982), p 294.

Discussion

Dr. William S. Dudley, chair
Air Commodore Henry A. Probert, RAF, Retired

Question: I feel like a prostitute in church. I realize that the honorable speaker probably believes he is talking to Bomber Command U.S.A., but I am a retired naval officer and not an aviator. I remember naval officers being trained only as sailors. In the early days of World War II, back in the summer of 1942, the only way the B–17s found their way to Kiska and Attu in the Aleutians was by being escorted by old PBYs piloted by naval officers who knew where the hell they were going. Nobody questions the valor of aviators. The B–17 valor over Germany was unsurpassed in World War II; I can't imagine taking the casualties those fellows took. But in all honesty the principal contribution of the RAF in World War II was not the Bomber Command but was the Fighter Command that defended the bomber bases.

Probert: Most of that I wouldn't disagree with. War is a business to which a very large number of different forces and different arms contribute. The last thing I would do, for example, would be to underestimate the enormously important role of Coastal Command, much of it unsung throughout the whole war. It wasn't my objective this evening, obviously, to talk about the total war strategy and the total contribution of the RAF in war. My purpose was to relate to what Pete Copp was saying, and he had been concentrating very much on strategic bombing. If I were going to talk about the total contribution of the RAF in war, I would be giving a very different talk and certainly stressing the importance of the maritime role. Moreover I should certainly be giving full weight to the role of the Fighter Command in many, many ways, and referring, of course, to all the many other airpower roles. It isn't a simple matter. I think I did make the point that the Battle of the Atlantic was crucial to the bomber offensive. I hope you will agree that I am not really differing significantly with you, but that it wasn't my purpose to cover the whole scene.

Question: I understand that Group Captain Dudley Saward wrote an

authorized biography of Air Marshal Harris for publication after his death.*
Do you have any information on that?

Probert: The biography was commissioned about fifteen years ago. Group Captain Saward had been one of Harris's staff officers at Bomber Command for part of the war. Harris gave it his blessing on the strict understanding that it would not be published in his lifetime, and it has been sitting there on ice ever since. I would assume that it will appear very shortly. It certainly is an authorized biography. Whether it will be seen to be the definitive biography once it appears is another matter. I have not personally had the opportunity to read the manuscript. I have heard a few comments on it from other sources, but it would be quite improper for me to mention those at this moment. It will be worth reading, I am quite sure, but I have a feeling that the definitive biography will remain to be written.

Question: Solly Zuckerman has raised the question of the form of strategic bombing that should have taken place in World War II. Could you comment on that and the question of bombing the lines of communication as a way to win the war?[†]

Probert: It's not a subject about which I feel particularly expert. In my view, Zuckerman was thinking of this largely in terms of preparing for a land attack in which it was absolutely crucial that among other things you knocked out the enemy's communications. I doubt he was thinking of actually knocking Germany out by disrupting its communications and not following up with a full-scale invasion.

Question: Something that has always struck me, as a person who works a little bit outside the sphere of twentieth-century history, has been what appears to be the tremendous inflexibility of the youngest of the services regarding doctrine. You can see the Navy evolving, for example, in the relative decline of the gun club during World War II. You can see the Army changing its attitude on several occasions toward the proper uses of armor. Yet British and American airpower authorities remained committed to strategic bombing. It seems to have been almost an *a priori* article of faith. What I am wondering is, could anything have shaken the convictions of the Harrises, the Portals, and the Eakers?

Probert: Do you want another lecture? I find that a daunting question. There is so much that one could say. I am not sure that I would accept the basic premise that the other two services were as flexible as you imply. I think there

---

*This biography was subsequently published: Dudley Saward, *Bomber Harris: The Story of Sir Arthur Harris* (London and Garden City, N.Y., 1984).

[†]Solly Zuckerman (1904–), British professor of anatomy, served as a scientific adviser during World War II. He was a proponent of bombing rail yards. See his autobiography, *From Apes to Warlords* (London, 1978).

was a lot of inflexibility in their attitudes. Certainly the attitude of the British Army was, until just before the war, that they weren't going back onto the Continent. Their attitude toward developing armored warfare really doesn't suggest to me that they were any more flexible than perhaps you are suggesting we were.

Certainly it is true that the bomber doctrine was central to RAF thinking and, I think, to the thinking of the Air Corps in the years between the wars. We had the evidence of World War I, limited as it was. It had an immense impact, and people remembered—the first time that bombs had rained down on the center of London. It dominated the thinking. There was the belief that the bomber really would always get through. It was a convenient doctrine, too. We were seeking to deter aggression just as we have been doing with far, far stronger weapons ever since 1945.

But if it is argued that when we got into the war we were inflexible and we remained utterly committed to the bombing doctrine, I must remind you that we had to remain with the bombing doctrine because there really was no other way in 1940. I am absolutely and utterly convinced that in Britain's situation in June–July 1940 we had certain stark choices. We could come to terms with the Germans. Churchill was not going to see that happen—indeed none of us were. I remember it very clearly myself as a youngster at school, but old enough to know exactly what was going on. That was the last thing we were going to do. Or we could wage a kind of defensive war. And what hope would that give to the conquered countries in Europe? We were very, very much aware of what was going on in France, who had been our ally. The Free French were over with us, expecting us to do something for them, believing somehow things were going to come right, and looking to us—nobody else.

We in the Commonwealth had to do something. We couldn't stay totally on the defensive. And how did we go on the offensive with no army to go back and fight on the Continent? It had to be by strategic bombing, and to begin with strategic bombing was ineffective, as we now find, in an absolute military sense. But even so, in 1940 and 1941, it did a great deal for our own morale and for the morale of the people on the Continent, and we learned a great many lessons that we applied in 1942, 1943, and 1944. We had to do it, but don't let's say that we were inflexible.

While we were going on with the bombing, we were learning the hard way all the lessons about the employment of tactical air power in support of our armies in North Africa, the lessons that in fact we jointly used later on when we went back into northwest Europe. We had not had a doctrine for the employment of fighter aircraft in ground attack, though the French had thought we could use them in this way; that's one of the reasons why they

AIR LEADERSHIP

wanted all our fighters over in France in 1940. But we weren't trained for that role, though we had to learn it later.

There was a fair amount of flexibility as the war proceeded. We had to adapt; we had to learn. But under the pressure of war, you take the situation as you find it. So I am afraid I do not accept the premise of your question or the specific point you make.

Question: When Churchill went to the Casablanca Conference in January 1943, he went with a proposal to transfer American bombing to a night effort. How serious were Churchill and the RAF about this?

Probert: I don't think I can be really precise, because that would call for looking pretty closely at Churchill's own records, and I think we shall probably only get the full answer when we see the next part of Martin Gilbert's biography. It is certainly true that Churchill's attitude toward bombing, and to many other aspects of the war, did change from time to time. He was far from consistent in many of the things that he did. One can see it at the time of the Battle of France. And certainly in his attitude toward bombing, there were periods when he was firmly persuaded, and then he appears to have had second thoughts. It depended a bit on whom he was talking to at any particular time.

I am a great admirer of Churchill. The leadership that he displayed was absolutely critical to victory, but that admiration doesn't extend to believing that every time he was absolutely right. I think it must be said that there were a good many occasions on which our military leaders, particularly our airmen, appreciated the military realities and had to remind him regularly what was at stake. Portal, Slessor, and, indeed, Harris all felt that you had committed yourselves to going by day, using the methods that you had worked on. While we had our misgivings about it, we felt that it would be quite wrong for us to try to encourage you to go some other way, and we gave you full backing. Churchill, however, was probably a bit ambivalent.

Question: I would like to go back to the matter of strategic bombing. Strategic implies strategy; however, in most cases it implies industrial and political bombing, bombing of the enemy industry and bombing of the people to break their will. How good to hear you say that General Spaatz was intuitively confident that the British Fighter Command would break the German attacks. Fortunately he was right. It wasn't British industry that beat the Luftwaffe; it was the Fighter Command. It wasn't German industry that nearly broke the bomber attack on Germany; it was their fighter command. We really haven't come to grips with recognizing the fact that it was the fighters that in the end drove the Germans out of the skies, along with the bombers, of course. But why was everybody so slow in recognizing this matter of the fighters being so crucial?

PORTRAITS

Probert: It is terribly easy for us all looking back, isn't it, when we know what happened afterwards? But when things are happening for the first time—that's when you learn the lessons. Yes, Spaatz said he believed we were going to win in the Battle of Britain. He was familiar not just with the fighter aircraft that we had, but with all the radar and the control and reporting system which was going to enable those fighters to operate effectively. That, of course, was one of the key reasons why we did not send any more fighters to France in 1940. We could operate them effectively only over our own territory with our control system. Until the battles had actually occurred, I suppose you couldn't be sure. It was the first time round. Let us remember that before Dunkirk the Germans had never met an effective fighter opposition. On the other hand, though we had won the daylight battle, we had certainly not won by night.

The night offensive which the Germans waged against us was virtually unhindered through the winter of 1940–41, and only by mid–1941 were we beginning to make some effective interceptions. At the same time, of course, our own night bomber offensive against Germany in those early years—I suppose getting on into 1942—had relatively small losses. They were largely due to aircraft failing to find their way or, of course, to ground defenses. The effectiveness of night air defenses was something also that had to be proved for the first time. We and the Germans learned it roughly at the same pace.

So why didn't we learn more quickly? Well, simply because we were learning during the first time that such a conflict had ever happened in history.

Question: During the Battle of Britain, there was a controversy in the RAF between those who favored meeting each German air attack with a big wing of fighters and those who believed that squadrons needed the freedom to operate independently. Which was the better way?

Probert: I think the answer really is a bit of both. In the group which was right in the front line, there simply wasn't time to put big wings together. In the group farther back, there was more time. Essentially we were learning the tactics as we went along, and I don't really think one should come down firmly on one side or the other. Remember that the battle didn't go on for very long; the main fighting lasted only about two months. While I have great admiration for Dowding, it stems more from the way in which he prepared in the prewar years and fought very, very hard to retain the fighter force. I do not think, however, that he controlled his two group commanders as firmly as he should have done during the battle itself. But one has to be very, very careful of going for absolutes in this business.

AIR LEADERSHIP

Question: I asked Air Vice Marshal Johnnie Johnson* that question last Monday, and he answered exactly as you did.
Probert: A good recommendation.
Question: The argument has been made that the Germans lost the Battle of Britain precisely because they shifted from a military target—fighters and airdromes—to industrial and political-psychological targets. Would you care to comment on that?
Probert: There is an element of truth in it. There was certainly a failure on the German part to appreciate what were the critical points that they needed to attack. If they were to win air superiority, drive Fighter Command out of the sky, and thus prepare the way for an invasion, the critical targets were the coastal radars, which they had one go at; having destroyed one, they failed to appreciate their significance and thereafter left them alone. Effectively we were never without our eyes and ears. Had we been deprived of those, it could have been a different story.

Certainly when they went for the airfields, we were forced up in the attempt to defend them, and had they persisted, they might have made it. If you leave aside the coastal radars, our Achilles' heel was not so much the shortage of aircraft but the shortage of trained pilots. Had they continued to force us into combat, we were going to be hard-pressed.

One of their nighttime strikes was off target and they hit London. Whereupon we reasonably enough decided that if they were going to go for London we would have a crack at Berlin. That's where Bomber Command comes in—the attack on Berlin was not effective in terms of doing significant damage, but it was highly effective as far as hitting at German pride was concerned. They got very annoyed and irritated, which is something a military commander ought never to do. Their emotions got the better of them, they diverted their attack, and that gave us the relief we needed.

---

*Air Vice Marshal James Edgar "Johnnie" Johnson (1916–) was the leading British ace (38 victories) of World War II. He has written a book on the history of air-to-air tactics: *Full Circle* (London, 1964).

III. PATTERNS

Rear Adm. William A. Moffett
1869–1933

Using Admiral Moffett's experience as Chief of the Bureau of Aeronautics in the 1920s, Thomas C. Hone of the Naval War College examines leadership problems encountered when new technology intruded into an established bureaucracy. Networks of airmen, businessmen, and politicians grew around the new technology of air power. Lt. Col. Harry R. Borowski of the Air Force Academy discusses Air Force connections with businessmen in the late 1940s. By then the Air Force had separated from the Army, while naval air remained within the Navy. This session's chairman is a close student of how rivalry developed between the services. Brig. Gen. Alfred F. Hurley, USAF, Retired, is Chancellor of North Texas State University and biographer of Admiral Moffett's most renowned adversary, Billy Mitchell.—W.T.

Reflections

Alfred F. Hurley

In thinking about what happened yesterday in the opening session, as well as last night, it occurred to me that it might be useful to take another look at a few points. We did examine a very special person in the evolution of the Air Force, Gen. Carl Spaatz, and then last night Air Commodore Henry Probert talked about American airmen in the context of service abroad and interaction with Royal Air Force counterparts. The discussions yesterday identified certain characteristics of air leaders. By no means can the list be definitive, and I would be the first to point out that across my own Air Force service I noted a tendency on my own part—and I suspect that it is true of all of us—to be autobiographical when talking about the characteristics of leadership.

Dr. Alfred Goldberg noted the importance of a sense of humor, of not taking oneself too seriously. Again I could get autobiographical. One of my first impressions when I joined the Air Force back in 1950 was that almost to a man among those under whom I served, there was this tendency not to take oneself too seriously. I thought it made service in the Air Force all the more attractive.

General LeMay emphasized a sense of responsiblity. I think all of us who heard him were reminded of our own experiences. Many could recall from officer training days having to memorize a definition of leadership that included the words "the eager acceptance of responsibility." Last night as I came up the stairs to the dining room in the officers' club here at Bolling, I noticed the pictures of a series of individuals who shaped the Air Force—Mitchell, Spaatz, Arnold, Rickenbacker, and Twining. If there is a theme that could be used to link individuals as different as they were, it was that they did eagerly accept responsibility.

Airmen like these prepared themselves for the responsibility of leadership as best they could. A few years ago at the National Archives I found a list of the men in the Air Corps who had the most flying hours. I was struck by the correlation between the names on that list and those who went on to positions of great importance in World War II and afterwards.

AIR LEADERSHIP

Last night we looked at air leadership in the context of international relations. This morning's discussion will unfold in the context of interservice relations. Because of illness, Adm. Thomas H. Moorer* could not be with us. You can really measure the change in attitudes among the services when you consider that just before Admiral Moorer retired from active duty, the Wings Club of New York gave him the Billy Mitchell Award.

---

*Ed. note: Adm. Thomas H. Moorer (1912–), a naval aviator, was Chief of Naval Operations (1967–70) and Chairman of the Joint Chiefs of Staff (1970–74).

Navy Air Leadership: Rear Admiral William A. Moffett As Chief of the Bureau of Aeronautics

Thomas C. Hone

The U.S. Navy has worked and fought at the leading edge of military technology for most of the twentieth century. That it did so successfully after World War I, a time when funds for equipment and personnel were limited in a way which might be considered irresponsible today, was due in large part to the ability of senior officers and their ambitious juniors to recognize and adopt technological innovations. The best of those officers understood that the peacetime Navy should develop doctrine, procure equipment, and train personnel to blunt any enemy attack in the opening weeks and months of a likely war and lay the foundations for ultimate victory. The need for officers with such foresight was especially great in 1919, because during World War I several new technologies showed significant promise in the field of naval warfare; foremost among these were the submarine, the airplane, and the wireless or radio. After the war, the Navy faced the challenge of integrating these new weapons into its organization and doctrine. A mission had to be defined for each. Funds had to be secured to purchase existing models of each device and to promote the development of newer, superior types. A means had to be devised to promote and review the the performance of the personnel who operated and maintained the new equipment. Much of this work had been done during World War I, but then cost had been no obstacle, and any weapon which appeared to have military utility was tried. After the war, the situation changed drastically. In 1919, visionaries were predicting publicly that the new military and naval technologies would displace existing equipment and tactics. At the same time, there were intense and widespread pressures in Europe and the United States to slash military expenditures. The future of the new technologies was uncertain.[1]

The growth of specifically Navy aviation programs during World War I was spectacular. In January 1914, when the Navy opened its first flying school at Pensacola, Florida, there were 9 officers, 23 enlisted men, and 7 aircraft in Navy aviation.[2] By the end of World War I, U.S. Naval Aviation Forces had increased to approximately 7,000 officers, 33,000 enlisted men, and over 2,100 aircraft.[3] This fantastic growth was followed by a rapid decline due to demobilization. By the early summer of 1919, the number of

AIR LEADERSHIP

officers in naval aviation was down to 580 (and only 370 of them were fliers), and the number of enlisted personnel had dropped to 4,879 (of whom 3,479 had aviation ratings).[4] World War I had demonstrated the importance of military aviation. There was no consensus in the Navy, however, concerning the best way of exploiting the potential of airplanes and rigid and nonrigid airships. Money, physical resources, and personnel available for naval aviation were limited. To get money for base construction, training, the purchase of new types of planes, and, above all, the construction of seaplane tenders and aircraft carriers, the Navy would have to reduce the money it could spend on completing the massive 1916 ship construction program—major elements of which had been deferred in favor of more pressing emergency construction (destroyers for example) during the war.

It was a time of uncertainty, change, and growing competition for scarce resources between the Army and Navy and among the branches of the two services. More was at stake than money. Navy aviators, convinced of the power and potential of their arm because of their war experience, promoted the claim that their technology would replace the gunnery which was the *raison d'etre* of the surface fleet. Brig. Gen. William "Billy" Mitchell, who had led the Army's air squadrons in France in World War I, had even stronger views: air power, he claimed, would soon make obsolete both the surface Navy and the massed infantry and artillery formations which had fought in France. Mitchell wanted a separate military department for aviation, and he and his supporters maintained that the forces which this department could develop would supplant (not merely support) the Army and Navy. The stage was set for intense and bitter organizational and political conflict. It was just the place for William A. Moffett.

In the paragraphs which follow, my main focus will be on Moffett—on his political and bureaucratic campaigns to further the status of naval aviation and to keep his place as its chief. At the same time, however, I will try to lay the foundation for a more general discussion of leadership—a topic I will consider in closing.

When Moffett was promoted to Rear Admiral and made Chief of the newly created Bureau of Aeronautics (BUAER) on July 25, 1921, he was no stranger to aviation. His association with pilots and planes began when as a captain, he commanded the Great Lakes Naval Training Station for four years before and during World War I. While in the post, Moffett met and cultivated the friendship of prominent Chicago businessmen and politicians, particularly William Wrigley, the chewing gum magnate. Moffett persuaded Wrigley to finance the Great Lakes Aeronautical Society and to accept the post of Society president. In turn, Wrigley sponsored and helped finance a variety of aviation-related activities at the station including a special Aviation Mechanics School for enlisted recruits. The school was not authorized by Josephus Daniels, the Navy Secretary, but Daniels, after inspecting it, agreed that the Navy would fund it fully. By the Armistice in 1918, about 3,500 mechanics had been dispatched by the school to Navy fields and bases; students and staff totaled 5,000 in November 1918, and the school had its own flying unit.[5] Moffett had achieved much while in charge of Great Lakes. The station graduated almost half of the Navy's enlisted personnel who served in World War I. Moffett also made a name for himself in aviation; as he wrote to Wrigley soon after his appointment as BUAER Chief, "it was my association with aviation there [at Great Lakes] that made me a candidate for this place."[6] Finally, Moffett—not a native of the region—made many influential friends while he built up the Great Lakes establishment. Wrigley was the most prominent and influential, but he was not the only one.[7]

After the war Moffett left Great Lakes and took a major seagoing command: battleship *Mississippi*, commissioned in December 1917. He had the crew rig places for hoisting and stowing spotter aircraft.[8] After two years with *Mississippi*, Moffett was chosen Director of Naval Aviation, a position in the Office of the Chief of Naval Operations (CNO). By that time, he had extensive experience with aviation at sea. The half year or so as Director of Naval Aviation gave Moffett the chance to convince both active fliers and his senior Navy colleagues that he was the right choice as BUAER Chief. Moffett did not emerge as a public figure at this time. Behind the scenes, he helped draft the general order which specified the responsibilities and powers of the new bureau.[9] The public campaign to create the new organization was pushed by others. Moffett waited until the powers of his office were set forth before moving aggressively to promote Navy aviation. From 1921 until his death in the crash of *Akron* in 1933, however, he sought center stage. He had honed his skills as an organizer, publicist, and politician at Great Lakes, and he used them to great effect as head of BUAER. As historian W.R. Braisted has noted, "Much of the early success of naval aviation must be attributed to Moffett."[10]

Yet Moffett was not alone in his advocacy of Navy aviation. He had powerful allies, both within the Navy and in Congress. In fact, some of the most important decisions about the future of naval aviation were made in 1919 while Moffett was captain of *Mississippi*. Before considering Moffett's years as BUAER Chief, the actions taken in 1919 need to be explored in some detail. Understanding them is essential if Moffett's later successes as BUAER Chief are to be explained. With demobilization, the Secretary of the Navy had to prepare a program for fiscal year 1920 and also decide how to distribute

AIR LEADERSHIP

the funds which were available for fiscal year 1919. There had to be some rationale behind the expenditure of existing funds and the request for future authorizations. As was customary at the time, the Secretary turned to the General Board of the Navy for its recommendations. The General Board was a panel of senior officers who were responsible for reviewing ship designs and strategic issues brought before them by the major Navy administrative divisions (the bureaus—mainly Ordnance, Navigation, Steam Engineering, and Construction and Repair). The Board was empowered to conduct studies and hold secret hearings in its efforts to reach a decision. After the war, the Board assumed that the 1916 building program would be completed. But it was not at all clear how the development of naval aviation would affect the 1916 authorizations.

In March 1918, the Office of the Director of Naval Aviation was made a part of the CNO's staff; the Director reported to the CNO and could use his access to forcefully present his views on the material and manpower needs of naval aviation.[11] However, the Director had no control over the major bureaus which supplied manpower or material to aviation units. Neither, for that matter, did the CNO. Indeed, before the Bureau of the Budget was created in 1922, the bureaus sent their separate budget recommendations directly to the Secretary of the Navy. The CNO and the Commander-in-Chief U.S. Fleet had only indirect control over the bureaus; their powers were largely confined to the field of operations. In the area of ship characteristics, however, the CNO could use his position as a nonvoting member of the General Board to influence the bureaus because the General Board had the official responsibility for determining the major military characteristics (speed, size, range, firepower) of Navy ships.[12] After the war, the CNO, Adm. W.S. Benson, refused to carry to the Board the request of Navy aviators that a special bureau or a separate corps be created for Navy aviation alone. He did not want Congress to create another organization in the Navy over which the CNO would have no direct control. Notwithstanding his reservations, the General Board began 1919 with an extended inquiry into the organization of and prospects for Navy aviation.

In the course of the General Board's investigation, Navy aviators presented and criticized their own views about the potential and proper organization of fleet aviation. All of the following major issues were considered:

1. Whether there should be a separate air service modeled on the RAF, or a separate air corps within the Navy, or a separate Bureau of Aeronautics.

2. If the last, then whether the new bureau should be given both material and operational responsibilities.

3. How, in doctrinal terms, aviation should be integrated into the Fleet.
4. How naval aviators should be recruited, trained, and promoted.
5. What sorts of aircraft should be purchased, and in what numbers.
6. Whether aircraft carriers should be constructed. Behind this issue stood one more fundamental: whether naval aviation should rely primarily on seaplanes or carrier-based aircraft.
7. The number of permanent airfields the Navy should have, and whether one should be set aside as a testing station for developing new weapons and tactics.
8. Whether the needs of Marine Corps aviation were significantly different from those of Navy aviation.
9. Whether the development of naval aviation by potential enemies could be offset by the construction of large numbers of aircraft and the ships to carry them. In other words, whether the use of scouting and attack planes at sea could give the advantage to a force operating without the cover of land-based aircraft.

Formal, secret hearings on these issues consumed most of the Board's time in 1919.

Contrary to what one might expect, support for an organized, well-funded naval aviation program was expressed by a number of influential senior officers. Rear Adm. Hugh Rodman, who had commanded the American battleship squadron which served with the British Grand Fleet, and Adm. H.T. Mayo, Commander-in-Chief of the U.S. Fleet during the war, both appeared before the Board to testify on behalf of a well-organized and financed Navy air service. Both were asked to appear because they had witnessed the operation of aircraft and lighter-than-air craft in wartime conditions. Both cited British and German experience, and both favored and urged the construction of aircraft carriers for strike missions.[13]

The Board also interviewed a number of Navy aviators, particularly those with experience in France. There were only two issues which divided them: (1) the question of whether most of the Navy's aircraft should be seaplanes or planes based on carriers, and (2) whether there should be a special "corps" of aviators in the Navy or only a Bureau of Aeronautics. Those who favored seaplanes over carrier- or land-based aircraft argued that seaplane bases could be constructed quickly in the event of war and that, with a reasonable expenditure of funds, the fleet could carry its planes with it and recover them after they were deployed. The seaplane advocates drew their conclusions about the future from the immediate past, when seaplanes had been used to patrol large areas of ocean. Along with proponents of the rigid airship, the seaplane sponsors thought that the best way to employ fleet aviation was in antisubmarine patrol, scouting, and gunfire spotting. Large

AIR LEADERSHIP

seaplanes or flying boats would, in company with airships, conduct extended reconnaissance missions. Smaller seaplanes, flying from tenders steaming with the fleet, would perform tactical scouting; floatplanes from battleships and cruisers would spot gunfire.

The majority of the regular aviators who had seen combat in France favored carrier-based aircraft, however, and they did so because they had witnessed British work with both carriers and seaplanes and had decided that the advantage lay with the former. As Cmdr. Kenneth Whiting, who had commanded the first U.S. naval air station in England, pointed out to the Board:

> If the war had gone on a little longer, the bombing of Kiel, Cuxhaven, and Wilhelmshaven would have been done from airplane carriers. The *Furious* was equipped with airplanes and made an attack on Tondern, as she steamed up and down the North Sea without hindrance.[14]

He and others also noted that seaplanes could never fly as fast or maneuver as well as land-based or carrier-based aircraft, which meant that, in a fleet engagement, the side with the higher performance aircraft could sweep the other side's planes from the air. In other words, the only real counter to a carrier was another carrier or shore-based aircraft—not seaplanes.

Those testifying on behalf of carrier aviation faced one logical dilemma: if they pressed their case for a carrier too hard and touted it as a strike weapon, then they could be forced to admit that, pushed to its limits, the argument for carriers was in fact an argument against a strong surface fleet whose primary weapon was the gun. Visionaries were quite willing to take that step. Adm. W.S. Sims, newly appointed head of the Naval War College and *ex officio* member of the General Board, did take that positon publicly as part of his effort to pressure the Navy toward a stronger commitment to sea-based aviation. Cmdr. J.H. Towers, one day to become head of the Bureau of Aeronautics, appeared before the General Board in March 1919, two months before he participated in the first trans-Atlantic air crossing, and he too presented the visionaries' case. When asked about the feasibility of planned, long-term aviation development programs, he responded:

> I don't think we can continue beyond . . . 1925 . . . in building aircraft carriers, because I think it will be quite possible that ships will all become more or less aircraft carriers and be so designed. . . . I should say the development of aviation is so startling that anyone is foolish if he attempts to lay down a six-years' aviation program.[15]

Most of the aviators who testified before the Board deliberately refrained from presenting positions as extreme as those taken by Towers. When they did not, they were taken to task by members of the Board; as one Board member commented, rather sarcastically:

> If you could point to something . . . that has been done in the North Sea, say, in the attack on Helgoland, or the north coast of Germany successfully carried out with 15 or 20 carriers, it would be very helpful.[16]

The Board returned again and again to specific questions: what types of planes should be built, how should pilots be trained and promoted, and how should aviation be organized within the Navy? As a senior member of the Board reminded a witness, "We are discussing the question of an organization within the Navy Department which will further the interests of aviation."[17]

At least the Board did not hear the aviators say they wanted a unified air service modeled after the RAF. As a former Director of Naval Aviation put it in March 1919:

> ... the urgent thing is to go ahead with the development of the use of aircraft with the fleet proper, particularly now when the move is for a united air service, and we strengthen our hand every time we can show that we are using it with the fleet.[18]

General Mitchell of the Army Air Service appeared as a witness before the Board, and he very politely but firmly informed the members that a unified air service was inevitable. The Board received different counsel from Navy fliers and higher commanders. Admiral Mayo put it best when he said:

> ... it is not at all a matter of whether we follow the British lead or not, but whether after due consideration of all the essential facts and bearings of the subject we adopt a correct policy.[19]

The General Board agreed. Though there were disagreements within the Navy over the proper form and use for aviation *with the fleet*, there was a consensus—shared by nonaviators as well as by the fliers—that British experience with naval aviation had shown the way: all forms of aviation at sea (dirigibles, carriers, and seaplanes) should be pursued vigorously.

In the course of its 1919 hearings, the General Board considered all the major tactical and organizational problems confronting naval aviation and even some of the technological problems of employing aircraft at sea. The proper role and authority of a bureau of aviation were thrashed out, alternate ways of procuring planes and then testing them were weighed. The personnel problem was obviously serious. There had to be some way of allowing aviators to specialize without placing their chance for promotion at risk. An "Aviation Duty Only" category—similar to the existing Engineering Duty Only specialization—was proposed and then criticized on the grounds that it would organizationally isolate aviation from the rest of the Navy.[20] At the end of its deliberations, the Board prepared a memo to the Secretary of the Navy. A number of its conclusions and recommendations were significant and influential, including the following:

> (a) ... fleet aviation must be developed to the fullest extent. Aircraft have become an essential arm of the fleet. A naval air service must be established, capable of accompanying and operating with the fleet in all waters of the globe.
>
> (b) Fleet engagements of the future will probably be preceded by air engagements. The advantage will lie with the fleet which wins in the air. ... airplane carriers for the fleet (should) be provided in the proportion of one carrier to each squadron of capital ships. ...

* * * * * *

AIR LEADERSHIP

(j) Development of all types of aircraft . . . and fleet aviation are the most important work for the immediate future. Construction should be kept as low as possible . . . but for experimental and development work, a liberal appropriation should be included in each yearly program.[21]

Some of the recommendations of the Board (such as its endorsement of an expensive rigid airship program) turned out later to be unwise. However, the overall theme of the document proved perceptive, and the Board's forthright stand on the side of an ambitious, organizationally integrated naval aviation program made it impossible for later opponents of naval aviation—especially General Mitchell—to halt its development.

Yet the Board did not recommend the formation of a special bureau for naval aviation. A new organization was needed. The Office of the Director of Naval Aviation had no separate budget authority; neither could it *directly* control the development of air doctrine. In consequence the Director of Naval Aviation was, as one aviation officer informed the General Board, "really without status."[22] To forestall any strengthening of the office, Admiral Benson further weakened it *after* the General Board had presented its June report to the Secretary recommending just the opposite. Despite Benson's action, the aviators did get their bureau and it was given the necessary authority, but the process took two years and concerted action both within the Navy and without.

Support for a bureau from outside the Navy was energetically given by a few key members of Congress, notably Rep. Frederick C. Hicks (Republican, New York) of the House Naval Affairs Committee. While the Wilson administration was still in the White House, support also came from both the Secretary and the Assistant Secretary of the Navy. Opposition came from General Mitchell of the Army, from three of the existing Navy bureaus (Ordnance, Navigation, and Engineering), and from senior Navy officers who feared that the creation of a new bureau would establish yet another semi-independent directorate within the Navy Department. Much of the opposition was political or emotional; some was sensible. It was not clear, for example, just how the proposed bureau could be staffed with a sufficient number of officers experienced in aviation. Mitchell feared that the Navy would pack the new bureau with nonaviators and simply waste money that a unified air service could spend more productively. Contrary to many claims made by its proponents at the time, military aviation was expensive. Individual aircraft and their weapons were not very costly, but the construction of airfields, repair shops, and aircraft carriers did take a great deal of money. According to historian Charles Melhorn, aviation's share of Navy appropriations was steady between 1922 and 1925 while the total Navy budget fell by twenty-five percent.[23] Military spending was bound to decline just when military aviation was going to need a larger and larger share of the available funds. Something had to give. It is no wonder that there was opposition (both within the Navy and without) to the creation of the new bureau.

But that opposition was not enough to check the movement toward a new organization for naval aviation. In February 1920, Rear Adm. D.W. Taylor, Chief of the Bureau of Construction and Repair, had a bill creating a new bureau drafted and then approved by the new CNO. Representative Hicks presented the bill in his committee, and in April of that year the committee held a series of hearings where the general issues were aired. According to an unpublished study by Clifford Lord, the only positive consequence of the 1920 congressional hearings was the abandonment by naval aviators of a claim to a special "corps" status within the Navy.[24] General Mitchell promoted the concept of a separate aviation "corps" to distinguish aviation as a special military activity; in so doing, he forced naval aviators to choose between a "corps" and staying "Navy." They chose the latter. Congress failed to approve the proposed legislation, but the existence of the bill gave the Navy an alternative to the measures then under congressional consideration which would have created a unified air service.

Behind the scenes, the General Board was slowly backing toward a position in favor of a separate bureau for naval aviation. The Board had the responsibility for recommending the designs of ships *and* aircraft to the Secretary of the Navy. The Board left detailed ship design issues to the bureaus, but it reserved to itself the right to specify the primary military characteristics which governed the balance of warship designs.[25] In 1920, the Board tried to do the same with proposed aircraft designs. In the case of warships, the Board would set gun size, armor thickness, endurance, speed, and tonnage. The Bureau of Construction and Repair would use such specifications as the basis of several alternative designs—from which the Board would, with the concurrence of the Bureaus of Ordnance and Steam Engineering, choose the "best" one. The Board tried to find factors similar to endurance, gun size, and armor thickness which would apply to aircraft. The effort was not successful. Aircraft designs were an even tighter compromise than ship designs; a slight change in one of the factors could produce major changes in one or more of the others. To compound the problem, the Board did not have before it a clear statement of aircraft doctrine. The deficiency was most serious in the case of aircraft for the carrier which both the CNO and the Secretary of the Navy had asked Congress to authorize. The sizes and weights of fighters, scouts, and attack planes would shape the design of the carrier; the carrier, if designed before the aircraft, might so limit the planes that they would not be capable of performing their military functions. As one

AIR LEADERSHIP

of the members of the Board pointed out, "you won't be able to get a plane until you get a ship, and we cannot design a ship without the plane."[26]

The Board wrestled with the task of specifying the military characteristics for aircraft all through 1920. Its deliberations were marked by complaints by the members: they did not know enough about planes or about flying to have the confidence to set aircraft characteristics; they could not anticipate the military potential of large, long-range airships; they did not want to recommend that Congress authorize carriers which would not operate future aircraft types. The Board was handicapped by a lack of experience in the fleet with aviation. Its efforts were also impeded because there was no one office which designed aircraft and their equipment. Construction and Repair (C&R) was responsible for aircraft structure, but the relationship between a plane's engine, its structure, and its performance was so tight that the designers in C&R could not draw up alternative aircraft designs in the same manner that they could and did produce alternate ship designs. To exercise competently its responsibilities in the field of aircraft design, the Board would have to create an organization which could pool the expertise of the bureaus and prepare aircraft designs the way the Preliminary Design Section of C&R produced ship designs. The alternative was to get out of the field entirely—to give one bureau the responsibility for aircraft design and production.

Thus did public pressure to create a new bureau receive strong but indirect support from the confidential labors of the General Board. Historians of this period of Navy aviation have missed this point. They have emphasized the growth of support outside the Navy for a new bureau in 1921. In April 1921, for example, the National Advisory Committee on Aeronautics (NACA) endorsed the concept of the special bureau, as did both President Harding and Edwin Denby, his appointee as Navy Secretary. These actions were no doubt crucial. But so, too, was the growing conviction by the General Board that the work of the new bureau would not compete with or hamper its own. The General Board became the most important silent proponent of a new bureau, and the Board's experience was evidence supporting the efforts by the new bureau's sponsors to give it "cognizance" over the process of aircraft design.

The new Bureau of Aeronautics (BUAER) survived and prospered for four reasons: (1) the energy and intelligence of its personnel, (2) the commitment made to aviation *in the fleet* by senior Navy officers, (3) the powers formally given the new organization in Navy regulations, and (4) the political perspicacity of Moffett. The depth of the Navy's commitment to aviation has already been described. In 1921, it was based on evidence of the value of aircraft scouting and spotting. Tests had shown that battleships could effectively use their heavy caliber guns at maximum range *only* with the support of aircraft spotters. Exercises had also demonstrated that aircraft were essential for long-range reconnaissance. There was no evidence that planes carried by aircraft carriers could sweep existing surface forces from the seas. Ambitious young aviation officers such as J.H. Towers, B.G. Leighton, H.C. Mustin, and Kenneth Whiting believed that their arm would soon provide that evidence, but Moffett understood that other needs were more pressing.

At least he had, on paper, most of the organization that he and the fliers had campaigned for. The new bureau's authority was impressive: "all that relates to designing, building, fitting out, and repairing Naval and Marine Corps aircraft," as well as the preparation of the bulk of the budget for naval aviation procurement, training, and support enterprises (airfields, shops, hangars, etc.).[27] The bureau also had "authority to recommend to the Bureau of Navigation and the Commandant of the Marine Corps" how pilots would be selected, assigned, and promoted.[28] As Lord noted in his detailed history of BUAER, Moffett had no intention of operating a purely material bureau; Moffett understood from the beginning that the success of BUAER would hinge on having enough money, enough men, and enough planes.[29]

Navy General Order Number 65 implemented congressional legislation creating BUAER and gave it authority not granted the older bureaus, but that authority was not unambiguous; it was couched in language which made possible either the assertion of authority or a retreat from it. Moffett, who drew up much of the order, was much too clever to attack directly the authority held by the Bureau of Navigation over the Navy's personnel, but his phrasing set the stage for a serious conflict between BUAER and Navigation in the later 1920s. The order directed the new bureau to supply the Chief of Naval Operations with all the information he might need regarding "all aeronautic planning, operations, and administration."[30] The order gave the new organization the following assets:

1. A wide scope of authority, covering (a) the procurement and testing of aircraft and their power plants, (b) training of pilots and mechanics, (c) study of new aircraft designs, (d) assigning aviation personnel to duty at sea and shore, (e) publicity, and (f) drawing up the budget for aviation in the Navy.
2. The tools to implement this authority, including the power to prepare a budget, a flag officer as bureau chief, and a mandate to work closely with the Chief of Naval Operations.

The political cost of all this was minimal: BUAER's chief had to qualify as an aviator or observer within a year, and not more than thirty percent of the new bureau's personnel who failed to qualify as pilots or observers could stay with

AIR LEADERSHIP

BUAER longer than a year after its creation. The statute authorizing BUAER did not designate carriers as commands for aviators, but it did direct that command of all Navy flying units be given to qualified aviators.[31]

Moffett had two immediate tasks: ward off the campaign waged by General Mitchell against a separate Navy air service, and plan the future of naval aviation. The first task took Moffett to Congress, to organizations like the American Legion, and to the press. The second task demanded a different attitude and a different approach. As Moffett wrote to Admiral Sims:

> We are getting up a plan for Fleet aviation, which will cover the next five years, and this is to be submitted to the General Board for approval. We are trying above all else to get Aviation afloat.[32]

Moffett wanted and needed the political and intellectual support of Sims to prepare and promote a plan for the long-range development of Navy aviation. Sims had contacts and prestige; as Commandant of the Naval War College, he was an *ex officio* member of the General Board. More important to Moffett was Sim's creation of a regular series of war games and simulations at Newport. Sims, former commander of U.S. Navy forces in Europe during World War I, did not intend to be exiled to the Naval War College prior to retirement. An advocate of aviation with the fleet, he moved to implement a program of campaign and battle simulations first suggested by Navy reformers such as Rear Adm. B.A. Fiske in the decade before World War I. Sims was in need of an ally in Washington; Moffett needed allies anywhere. The War College simulations soon suggested that carriers could indeed play a powerful role in naval warfare; Moffett was quick to feed ideas and information to Sims. It was not simply a matter of prudence on Moffett's part to cultivate Sims. Moffett had already decided that Sims had excellent judgment because the younger officers (such as H.C. Mustin, J.H. Towers and E.S. Land) who Sims had recruited as proteges had become assets for Moffett.[33] There was, with Moffett's approval, something of a Sims "mafia" in BUAER, and both Moffett and Sims profited from the arrangement.

General Mitchell was a more pressing concern. Mitchell's bomber crews had sunk the *Ostfriesland* on July 21, 1921, and the general had at once launched a public attack on the surface Navy. The sympathetic and supportive attitude which Army aviators had taken toward naval aviation when testifying before the Navy's General Board in 1919 had been replaced by one of public criticism. But Navy fliers understood that their service was organizationally committed to aviation. Proof of the strength of that commitment was the Navy's struggle in late 1921 at the Washington Naval Conference for adequate aircraft carrier tonnage and a special exemption that would allow the United States to convert two large unfinished battlecruisers to first-line aircraft carriers. By attacking the Navy, Mitchell was driving the Navy surface community closer to Navy aviators. Mitchell did not care. He proposed to create a U.S. Air Force modeled on the RAF, despite opposition from the Army, the Navy, and even from U.S. aircraft manufacturers.[34] The Army had originally made aviation part of the Signal Corps because of the obvious utility of air reconnaissance. The Army created a separate Air Service in World War I, and charged it with air support of existing ground and coast defense forces. Mitchell wanted a separate air department, and he maintained that the new department could take over the Navy's role of continental and colonial defense.

The story of Mitchell's crusade and court-martial is well known. Less well understood is the Navy's position, together with Moffett's role in the political battle against Mitchell. Moffett fought Mitchell in two places—Congress and the press. Beginning in 1921, Moffett promoted Navy participation in air races and air shows. He meant to show that the Navy could procure quality aircraft and train skilled pilots. His goal was to refute Mitchell's claim that the Navy cared little about aviation and could do little in the field even if it did care. Moffett also continued a process he had begun while head of the Great Lakes training station—cultivating support for his organization and for himself among the politically influential. The Mitchell-Moffett struggle pit publicist against publicist, political sophisticate against political sophisticate.

There were two differences, however, and they determined the outcome of the conflict. Mitchell did not have doctrinal and political support within the Army like that which Moffett had both inherited and then carefully cultivated within the Navy. Mitchell could not have it because his stated purpose was to dismember the Army. The second difference was based on different interpretations of the facts. Mitchell claimed that an air offensive, properly directed and supported, could be strategically decisive, even at sea. But his position did not rest on reliable data. It was true, for example, that an airplane could launch one torpedo and disable a battleship, but the Navy well knew that juxtaposing the cost of the battleship with that of the plane and torpedo was an unfair comparison. Torpedo planes were slow, their range was limited, and they had trouble navigating (let alone attacking) in poor weather (to say nothing of darkness). Moreover, torpedo planes were extremely vulnerable in their final run against a target, and there was always the chance that an enemy would destroy them on the ground or on their carriers with his own light bombers before they were even launched. There was no effective observation/air defense fighter coordination system in 1921—or even in the United States in 1941. Moreover, planes had relatively short ranges; the only effective way to defend them on the ground was to hide or disperse them, and dispersion made launching mass attacks very difficult. Finally, aviation was *not* cheap. Behind the bomber (carrying bombs or torpedoes) was an

AIR LEADERSHIP

organization of fields, maintenance depots, training stations and manufacturing centers. As Melhorn noted, Navy aviation's share of congressional appropriations for the Navy Department as a whole *increased* between 1922 and 1925 at the expense of other branches of the service, even though the Bureau of Aeronautics was not able in that period to produce a satisfactory program for supplying aircraft to the fleet.[35] Congress would not pay for a strong air service *and* a strong Navy and Army. Yet the Army and Navy dared not drop out some weapon (such as the battleship) or organization (such as the Coast Artillery) in the meantime to finance an aviation department over which they had no control.

There were additional non-political reasons why the Navy opposed a unified air service. One was that the Joint Army and Navy Board of Aeronautics (created in 1919) and the National Advisory Committee for Aeronautics (created in 1915) were effective institutions for limiting uneconomical redundancies of procurement and research in the Army and Navy. The evidence was strong that they already performed the functions which advocates of a separate air service claimed only a new agency could accomplish.[36] Moreover, the NACA was not convinced of the merits, from a research point of view, of unification. There was evidence, for example, that the quality of fundamental aeronautical research had deteriorated after the RAF had assumed the responsibilities of the British counterpart to the NACA.[37] Another reason for Navy opposition to a unified air force was that such a force would probably neglect lighter-than-air development. The new BUAER chief had great hopes for long-range airships which would carry their own aircraft, but the Army had no faith in the Navy's program. The Army did not share the Navy's need for extended strategic reconnaissance—which was just another illustration of the different ways the Army and Navy used military aviation.

Moffett used these arguments against Mitchell, but only *indirectly*, by arguing that the Navy had indeed integrated aviation into the U.S. Fleet and that it had already reaped *tangible* benefits from doing so. Moffett carried this message to a variety of organizations and to Congress, and he used his many influential acquaintances, such as Porter Adams, Chairman of the American Legion's Aviation Committee in Massachusetts, to spread his theme. Moffett also developed the technique of handing off touchy questions to special committees. In April 1922, for example, he persuaded the NACA to appoint a technical committee to "pass upon the design and calculations" of airship ZR–1 (later the *Shenandoah*). The committee duly approved the design (as Moffett knew it would); it was "an astute political move" and one which Moffett was to employ again.[38] To complete his campaign against Mitchell, Moffett first had BUAER determine the functions and qualifications of naval aviation observers and then "recommend" to the Bureau of Navigation a course of training for that specialty. Navigation approved the course in March 1922, and Moffett qualified as an observer on June 17th, thereby blunting the charge that aviation in the Navy was controlled by men who had no experience as fliers. Moffett was no pilot like Mitchell, but he regularly flew his two-star admiral's flag from his aircraft (he was the first Navy flag officer ever to do so), and he spent hundreds of hours in the air to counter the attacks that he lacked "hands-on" experience in airplanes.

The struggle with Mitchell came to a head in 1924 and 1925. In the spring of 1924, a special Select Committee of the House of Representatives (the Lampert Committee) began an eleven-month investigation of national aeronautical policy. In testimony before the Committee, General Mitchell put his case strongly: "It is a very serious question whether air power is auxiliary to the Army and the Navy, or whether armies and navies are not actually auxiliary to air power."[39] Despite the fact that Mitchell's views were not those of the Army Air Service, Navy Secretary Curtis D. Wilbur established the Eberle Board, chaired by CNO E.W. Eberle, to clarify the Navy's position on aviation. The report of this board, issued in January 1925, was a slap at General Mitchell and his supporters in Congress: "it cannot be said . . . that air attack has rendered the battleship obsolete."[40] At the same time, Eberle and his colleagues recommended (1) a progressive, steadily funded aircraft building program, (2) completion of the converted battle cruisers *Lexington* and *Saratoga* as carriers, (3) authorization of a new, built-for-the-purpose 23,000-ton carrier, (4) a Naval Academy course in aeronautics, (5) "assignment of all qualified Academy graduates to aviator or observer training after 2 years of sea duty," and (6) creation of a Navy Department policy covering the assignment of officers to aviation.[41] This last recommendation gave Moffett the chance to appoint yet another board—composed entirely of aviators and headed by Capt. A.W. Johnson, the first commander of the large seaplane tender *Wright*. The Johnson Board recommended in April 1925 that the Navy Department train five times as many officers in aviation, create a Naval Reserve pilot program, and train enlisted personnel as pilots.[42] Thus was Moffett heading for a double showdown: with Mitchell and with the Navy's Bureau of Navigation.

In 1922 after a year as BUAER Chief, Moffett had sent CNO R.E. Coontz and Navy Secretary Edwin Denby a very important memo on Navy aviation policy. Coontz had strongly supported Moffett and had asked him to prepare a formal statement of the bureau's program. Moffett's response was both prescient and the beginning of a long conflict with the Bureau of Navigation. The memo's basic theme was that

> fleet aviation cannot successfully be expanded rapidly upon declaration of war; it is true that we can make a rapid increase in the production of aviation material, but

AIR LEADERSHIP

> experience has shown that a year of training and indoctrination is necessary for an aircraft squadron before it can operate in the fleet efficiently and safely.... Any normal individual can become a good flyer in a few months, but it takes years of other kinds of training in addition to flying to make that individual competent to perform aviation duty in the fleet.[43]

The memo then extended the argument for preparedness to peacetime conditions, citing the need to plan carefully so that the right number of trained pilots came together in the fleet with the necessary aircraft.

> The Bureau of Aeronautics can perform its duties . . . much more efficiently and economically if it can base its plans, material development, and personnel recommendations on a definite program . . . that extends several years ahead of each year's aeronautic appropriation.[44]

Moffett then used Mitchell's agitation against the Navy to bolster his argument for a sustained aviation program:

> In view of the revival of the agitation for a single air service, which is a constant and very real menace to the Navy's control of its aviation, it is imperative for the Department to be able to show that it is taking the most serious interest in the expansion of fleet aviation.[45]

Moffett also claimed that a definite program to expand "naval aviation afloat" would win Congressional support and benefit from economies of scale in manufacturing.

The Navy and Moffett were wrestling with the sticky problem of training aviators without isolating them from the rest of the fleet. There was an obvious need for pilots. But where would they go as they rose in rank? There would come a time when they could no longer fly. Giving them command of airfields and stations ashore was one way to employ more senior pilots (commanders and captains). They could also be given carrier commands. But how could their experience become a part of the fleet's generally? The solution was rotation: from Annapolis to sea duty, and from there to flight training at Pensacola; after a tour as pilot, an officer would then go back to sea as part of the regular Navy. As Moffett put it,

> if a constant increase in the number of Naval Aviators is decided upon, it will be possible immediately to make a plan for the return of aviators to general service duty after a fixed term of aviation duty; if such a plan is not evolved . . . we will soon have a Naval Flying Corps in fact if not in name, and this would weaken one of our strongest arguments against the single air department propagandists.[46]

To make this plan work, BUAER would need authority to draw large numbers of young officers from the fleet. In effect, BUAER would need to assume *de facto* control over a large area of Navy personnel policy.

This memo presented three elements of BUAER policy which formed the essence of Navy interwar aviation: an emphasis on training pilots as Navy aviators, the thousand-plane production program (or "hidden subsidy") to promote the aircraft industry, and the challenge to the Bureau of Navigation over the control of aviation personnel policies.[47] Admiral Moffett relied on General Mitchell's rhetoric to pressure Navy admirals who lacked a commitment to a strong aviation program. If critics of aviation argued that the military value of aircraft was not what its advocates claimed, Moffett could—and did—respond by saying that it was his way or Mitchell's way. And with the Navy behind him, Moffett could argue that results were forthcoming in aviation *without* a special, separate department of aviation. In 1923, for example, naval air units performed impressively in the annual fleet problem, and *Shenandoah* made its first flight. In 1924 *Langley*, the first carrier, operated regularly with the battle fleet for the first time, and *Shenandoah* first tied up to the airship mooring mast on the tender *Patoka*. Each month that passed made Navy aviation more secure. Mitchell had to move against Moffett before it was too late.

The crash of *Shenandoah* in September 1925 gave him his chance. Mitchell publicly charged that the destruction of the airship was caused by "incompetency, criminal negligence and almost treasonable administration of the national defense by the war and navy departments."[48] The charge cost him his career. It also led President Coolidge to create the President's Aircraft Board, headed by Dwight Morrow. The Morrow Board was a turning point in Moffett's career, and its decisions secured the future of naval aviation. After covering much of the ground already reviewed in detail by the House Select (Lampert) Committee, the Morrow Board issued a report on November 30, 1925—two weeks before the report of the Lampert Committee. The Morrow Board's conclusions affecting the Navy were:

1. That there was no need for an independent air force.
2. That procuring the same aircraft through one agency for both the Army and the Navy was unnecessary.
3. That Congress should create Assistant Secretaries for Aeronautics in both the War and Navy Departments.
4. That only naval aviators be given command of aircraft carriers and aviation stations ashore.
5. That Congress authorize a five-year, thousand-plane procurement plan.[49]

The report of the Lampert Committee was different; it recommended the creation of a unified defense department with a separate air service whose staff would hold positions on existing organizations such as the Navy's General Board and the Army's General Staff.[50]

The work of Moffett's Johnson Board had been criticized by the Bureau of Navigation as unfairly biased toward aviation. To counter his critics, Moffett persuaded the CNO to appoint yet another investigating committee, headed by Rear Adm. Montgomery M. Taylor, to review the issues which the Morrow Board was then considering. The report of the Morrow Board made the work of the Taylor inquiry unnecessary, however. The prestige of the former was such that Congress authorized the thousand-plane building

AIR LEADERSHIP

program, the aircraft-carrying airships *Akron* and *Macon*, the new position of Asssistant Secretary of the Navy for Aeronautics, and the rule which restricted carrier commands to aviators.[51] Admiral Taylor was then appointed to head a second board to map out specific goals of naval aviation over the next five years.

The second Taylor board had a strong impact on naval aviation policy. One reason Moffett had urged its creation was that he wanted a counterweight to the General Board. The General Board had begun criticizing BUAER policy during the course of its 1922 review of BUAER recommendations for alterations for *Lexington* and *Saratoga* and for carrier designs. The General Board had authority over every ship design produced by the Navy; the board reviewed alternative designs and sent its recommendations to the Navy Secretary. BUAER had been experimenting with aircraft-carrying submarines and destroyers, as well as with planes launched from airships. Studies first conducted at the Naval War College and subsequently confirmed in exercises had shown that numbers of planes were the key to control of the air. Other things being equal, the side with the most aircraft was the side which gained air superiority, and air superiority was essential to victory in daylight surface engagements against the Navy's most likely enemy, Japan.

Yet the Washington Naval Treaty had limited the United States to 135,000 tons of carriers. *Lexington* and *Saratoga* would eat up 66,000 tons of that—nearly half. Moffett and the Plans Division of BUAER wanted lots of small carriers; with a design of 13,800 tons, they could get five from the 69,000 tons allowed them by treaty. To supplement the carriers, BUAER proposed using battleship and cruiser floatplanes for reconnaissance and gunfire spotting, and equipping submarines and destroyers with aircraft. Moffett himself favored airship aircraft carriers such as *Akron* for long-range reconnaissance. BUAER's argument was that planes launched from platforms other than carriers would save carrier aircraft for combat missions—gaining air superiority and attacking enemy ships. The General Board did not oppose the concept of carrying the maximum number of aircraft with the fleet. The Board did resist the cost of doing it BUAER's way. The *Lexington* and *Saratoga* conversions were running behind schedule and over budget. Inefficiency was not the problem. Instead, BUAER was making changes in the design which cost money but which exercises on *Langley* had shown were essential. One example was the construction of bomb elevators and fueling stations on the flight decks of the two big carriers, a modification whose real worth was not demonstrated until World War II. The General Board was suspicious of BUAER's claims and its proposals. Moffett claimed that the battle cruiser conversions were extraordinary, but the Board was unmoved. It opposed construction of *Akron* and *Macon*, and turned down BUAER requests for aircraft-carrying submarines and destroyers.

Moffett was a master of using advisory boards. He used one in 1922 to sustain the airship program. He was persuasive and steady before the Lampert Committee and the Morrow Board. He used his own Johnson Board to force action on the matter of reserving carrier commands for aviators. The Taylor Board of 1926–27 was just as effective as any of these earlier efforts. Two of its brightest members were also carrier advocates: Capt. Joseph Mason Reeves and Capt. Harry E. Yarnell. They could be counted on, Moffett knew, to present a case for carrier aviation and to argue BUAER's case in a setting outside the restricted confines of the General Board.

The second Taylor Board was an unqualified success from Moffett's point of view. It set priorities among aircraft types and rejected the concept of multipurpose carrier aircraft. It also recommended airship development and the use of planes on submarines and destroyers. Finally, it endorsed the concept of the small carrier.[52] The General Board did not drop its opposition to aircraft-carrying destroyers and submarines, but it did accept BUAER's views on small carriers and it went along on airship development. The General Board also began backing down on its claim that it should specify what types of planes the Navy should buy.

BUAER emerged from the many hearings and reviews of the midtwenties in excellent condition. The Navy would keep its own air force and receive its own airships and aircraft carriers. The long-term aircraft procurement program was law, and a quantity of skilled pilots seemed possible with the establishment of a Naval Aviation Reserve. More importantly for Moffett, BUAER had successfully defended its organizational prerogatives. It retained responsibility for designing and procuring planes; it had cooperated quietly but successfully with both the Army and the NACA to improve aircraft designs and especially power plants. The bureau had also established and maintained close contact with fleet aviation. There was no division between users and suppliers as there was between, for example, the Bureau of Ordnance and users of Ordnance's products. Much of the credit for such close ties between line and staff was due personally to Moffett. When he was not on the move inspecting or touring or generating publicity, he was writing sincere and respectful letters of encouragement to officers such as Reeves who were actually making aviation a part of the fleet.

It was Reeves who had galvanized the *Langley*'s aviators in 1926 by asserting that the experimental carrier could operate three and a half times the twelve planes she then carried. Reeves had spent 1925 at the Naval War College, where the simulations established by Admiral Sims had persuaded him that carriers simply had to carry more aircraft. Reeves carried this lesson with him to the *Langley*. Over the opposition of her aviators, he increased the *Langley*'s aircraft complement to forty-two, and he insisted that both aircraft landing and launching intervals be slashed.[53] Within a few months, the landing interval for the *Langley*'s planes was down to thirty seconds; the equivalent interval on contemporary Royal Navy carriers was a good five minutes.[54] To get the landing interval down, Reeves had planes land and then move forward on the flight deck. To keep landing aircraft from piling into the planes parked forward, the *Langley*'s crew invented various crash barriers. The combination of new techniques and new equipment gave the U.S. Navy a clear lead in carrier aviation. As Reeves noted in a letter to Moffett in 1928,

> . . . Vice Admiral Fuller, R.N. . . . was in port for several days recently. Admiral Fuller manifested the keenest interest in our aviation. . . . While not an aviation man technically, he knows a great deal about it and I found his views extremely sound. He became . . . almost violent, in his denunciation of the present organization in England of the Royal Air Force. . . . I am quite certain from remarks which he made and his extreme surprise when I told him that we had operated 24 planes from the *Langley*, that the British Fleet does not approach our Fleet in the scope and probably efficiency of their Fleet operations. Of course I did not tell Admiral Fuller that we operated not 24, but 36 and could operate 42 and possibly 48 airplanes from the *Langley*.[55]

Reeves also saw to it that dive bombing became an accepted tactic among fleet aircraft squadrons. The letter from Reeves is revealing; it almost gloats over the dilemma of the Royal Navy. In it there is the shared pride of professionals who have together contributed to an achievement which, in the eyes of their major rivals, seems beyond possibility. Fostering this sense of shared triumph over serious odds was one of Moffett's goals; it worked—both for the Navy and for Moffett who gained the friendship of fleet officers whose support he would need to retain his post as BUAER Chief.

A subject of great importance to Moffett in 1924 and 1925 was his reappointment as BUAER Chief. Moffett was made a regular rear admiral in 1923, which meant he was eligible for a senior seagoing command. His first term as BUAER Chief was up in the summer of 1925. The question was, would he retire, go to sea, or remain in Washington? Moffett, then 57, wanted to stay where he was, and he could muster a strong argument for doing so. When the House Select Committee began taking testimony in the fall of 1924, *Langley* had not yet had a year with the fleet, and *Shenandoah* had only been flying a year. It was not an exaggeration to term Navy aviation still experimental, and it was not at all a sure thing that Navy aviation would survive as a part of the Navy. Moffett was undoubtedly effective with Congress and within the Navy. His skills as an advocate and a publicist were acknowledged. Yet the position of BUAER Chief was highly desirable. It was an appointment sent by the President to the Senate for its approval, and Moffett knew there were rivals for the post.

In November 1924, Moffett wrote to William Wrigley for aid:

> There are several candidates who are very active in their efforts to be appointed Chief . . . in my place, notably Captain Gherardi, U.S.N., now Aide to the Secretary. My information is that he is carrying on a very active and complete campaign for the appointment. . . . I am afraid that Gherardi and the other candidates will line up certain powerful people who will commit themselves . . . and also commit the Secretary and probably the President himself.
>
> * * * * * *
>
> If you feel you can, and are entirely willing to do so, I think your influence would have to be brought on the President. . . . [56]

In a February 1925 letter to Wrigley, Moffett was more explicit about the opposition to his reappointment:

> my attitude, especially in regard to publicity, has met the opposition and criticism of the older officers in the Navy Department, and I believe that they will oppose my reappointment. . . . I think it means that the question of my reappointment will be very carefully considered by the President, and that it will not be treated as a routine matter.[57]

Moffett had courted public attention. He approved of Navy fliers and machines competing in air races and setting records. There is evidence, for example, that Moffett even misused the airship *Shenandoah* by displaying her before the public and denying her crew the chance to work with the fleet.[58] In December 1923, Moffett was granted permission by Navy Secretary Denby and President Coolidge to employ *Shenandoah* in a trans-polar flight. Congress balked at the cost, however, and Coolidge cancelled the expedition in February 1924. But Moffett flew with *Shenandoah* on a highly publicized cross-country trip in October 1924, and General Mitchell was not that far off the mark when he charged (after her loss in 1925) that the use of the airship was irresponsible.[59]

Moffett won reappointment in 1925, and not only because he had friends in high places. He also moderated his previously strong advocacy of racing, despite his view that it was a valuable source of publicity. As a result, Navy fliers ceased competing in major international races after 1926. He had also gained the respect of many of the younger aviators, if only by trusting a number of them with important appointments. Cdr. H.C. Mustin was Moffett's aide in BUAER until Mustin was killed in a plane crash in August 1923; Mustin and Cdr. Kenneth Whiting, who had made the first catapult take-off (from *Langley*), argued strongly for carrier aviation. Lt. Cdr. B.G. Leighton headed the design division of BUAER and then served as aide to D.S. Ingalls, the Navy's only World War I ace and first Assistant Secretary of the Navy for Aeronautics. Leighton was also a strong advocate of carriers, and he prepared and delivered several influential lectures on the future of carrier tactics at the Naval War College in 1927 and 1928.[60] Moffett did not have to motivate the new bureau officers; rather the reverse—he had to demonstrate to them that his leadership was worth their support. He had plenty of talent working for him, including a number of young naval

AIR LEADERSHIP

engineers who were both bright and eager to apply their skills to aviation development.[61] Indeed, Adm. A.M. Pride, first to land and take off from *Lexington*, maintained that the aviators had in fact chosen Moffett "in cold calculation."[62] Whether that particular story is true or not, it is clear that Moffett trusted the talent and gave it support. This attitude paid double dividends: it encouraged innovation, and it won BUAER's chief the reputation he needed to hang on to his post.

The real crisis for Moffett came when Adm. C.F. Hughes was made CNO in November 1927. Rear Admiral Joseph Mason Reeves had persuaded Hughes of the great potential of naval aviation in 1926, when Hughes commanded the battle fleet, but Hughes was just as strong an advocate of the position that bureau chiefs should only serve four years. Indeed, as the historian W.R. Braisted has argued, the matters of principle and policy which quite legitimately divided Hughes and Moffett sometimes paled beside their personality differences.[63] Hughes was "old Navy"—reserved, discreet, intensely proud, professional, and self-effacing. Moffett was his opposite in almost all respects. At best, the two might respect one another; there was no way they could be friends. Their personal differences fueled their professional disagreements, and the result was harmful both to BUAER and the Navy.

Hughes' primary concern was that the bureau chiefs could resist the authority of the CNO by courting support in Congress. Hughes believed Moffett had done this, with serious negative consequences for the Navy. Largely because of Moffett's strong advocacy, for example, Congress authorized *Akron* and *Macon*, and Hughes believed that these airships drew scarce funds away from other more valuable aviation programs.[64] Hughes also sided with Rear Adm. R.H. Leigh, Chief of the Bureau of Navigation, when Leigh charged in April 1928 that BUAER personnel policies were causing unnecessary aviation fatalities. Moffett and Leigh had already clashed over the proper relationship between Aeronautics and Navigation. General Order No. 65, which had defined the authority of BUAER, had specified that

> the Bureau of Aeronautics shall make recommendations to the Bureau of Navigation for the detail of officers for duty in connection with aeronautics and shall make recommendation to the Bureau for the distribution in the various ratings of the enlisted personnel required for aeronautic duties. . . .[65]

The Morrow Board had gone one step farther and recommended that naval aviators be given posts in the office of the CNO and in the Bureau of Navigation. It was clear to Morrow and his colleagues that naval aviators were more than regular line officers with aviation training; their careers were different than those of regular seagoing officers. Navigation, however, had the responsibility for training naval officers first and specialists later.

It was an old problem which had never been solved. Moffett had argued before the General Board, the House Select Committee, and the Morrow Board that naval aviation was a part of the fleet and naval aviators were *not* part of a special corps or eligible for "limited duty only" like Navy doctors or some engineers. At the time of the Morrow Board hearings, however, Moffett had drafted for the Secretary of the Navy a special memorandum which put the case for an "Air Corps" organized parallel to the regular line of the Navy. The personnel of the new corps would have a separate promotion path, and their training would be controlled by the Navy's "Air Corps" or "Air Force," not by the Bureau of Navigation. The memo also tried to protect aviation officers from being forced into other duties:

> Officers of the Air Corps on sea duty [will perform] in general, duties similar to those performed at present by officers of the Line: but when operating in conjunction with aircraft their air duties will be paramount, and will be so arranged by commanding officers as to not be interfered with by other duties assigned.[66]

Such a recommendation undermined the authority of the Bureau of Navigation and of the CNO. Why Moffett wrote it is not clear. It might have been a means of pressuring the CNO to lean on the Bureau of Navigation. Or it might have been written in response to a CNO request for an outline of such an organization. Whatever its purpose, the fact that it was written shows how uncertain the organization and status of Navy aviation was in 1925—four years after the creation of BUAER. The Morrow Board steered clear of the "Air Corps" concept and promoted a cooperative solution to aviation's peculiar personnel problems. As Lord noted in his detailed BUAER history, BUAER and the Bureau of Navigation could and did work together, at least in 1927.[67] In 1928, however, the real issue was not personnel; it was Moffett and whether he would be appointed to a third term as BUAER Chief. With Hughes as CNO, Admiral Leigh apparently believed he could move successfully against Moffett. Personalities and service politics made inevitable a conflict between Moffett and Leigh. It was not simply a struggle between advocates and detractors of Navy aviation.

Moffett argued skillfully against the Bureau of Navigation position within the Navy Department. His position was that the Secretary of the Navy should not tamper with BUAER's original grant of authority as stated in General Order 65. Moffett treated the conflict as one which pit BUAER (and *not* himself) against senior admirals who did not comprehend the special personnel problems of naval aviation. Privately to his patron Wrigley, Moffett took the same position:

> The old timers in the Navy don't appreciate Aviation, and as a matter of fact I feel that the national defense is being jeopardized by their antagonism to Aviation. The jealously and envy of it is centered largely on myself, and they would get me out of here now if they could.[68]

AIR LEADERSHIP

Moffett beat back the Bureau of Navigation's challenge to BUAER personnel policies before a special inquiry (the Naval Aviation Personnel Inquiry or Standley Board) convened in May 1928. That October, Moffett solicited Wrigley's help to hold his post as BUAER Chief. He again couched his appeal in terms of naval aviation:

> The present Chief of Naval Operations, Admiral Hughes, and the Chief of Bureau of Navigation, Admiral Leigh, are antagonistic to me, I think because of my vigorous advocacy of Aviation and its importance. There is no question, in my opinion, that the whole Navy does not appreciate Aviation and its importance. . . . My work here has been one struggle and fight and still is.
>
> About six weeks ago I informed the Secretary . . . that the only logical place for me to go when I left my present position would be in command of the Aircraft Squadrons, Battle Fleet. . . . but Admiral Hughes and Admiral Leigh have stated that having been on shore so long I should not go to sea again but should take duty on the General Board or other shore duty. This is practically being put on the shelf . . . a thing that I greatly resent.
>
> I think practically everybody in Aviation in the Navy would be glad to see me stay where I am . . . I think I am safe in saying that I have the support of practically everybody in Naval Aviation.
>
> . . . I have called the Secretary of the Navy's attention . . . to the fact that . . . practically the only place for me to go is in command of the Aircraft Squadrons. My intention is to stand pat. . . .
>
> . . . Many think that owing to my knowledge not only of the operation and administration of the Bureau of Aeronautics but on account of my contact with Congress, my known ability to obtain money from the Budget and from the Appropriations Committees of both Houses is a great asset. . . .
>
> . . . The reasons for my remaining are . . . what I have told you and those that you yourself thought of when you spoke to Mr. Coolidge on my behalf . . . in other words, the sound business reasons which you gave him.
>
> . . . I can not carry on any real campaign in the matter until after the election. Of course there is no reason why my friends who believe I should remain here should not speak to the President or even to Mr. Wilbur. . . . [69]

There was the argument: keeping him on made sense economically, administratively and politically, and Navy aviators favored it. Moreover, it was either BUAER chief or command of the battle fleet's aircraft squadrons, where Moffett would become eligible for a three-star command.

In a December letter to Capt. E. S. Land, the assistant chief of BUAER, Moffett was more direct:

> efforts made for my reappointment will have to concentrate on Mr. Wilbur as well as on Mr. Hoover, and both will have to be done. . . . Mr. Wilbur will be influenced probably by men like Senator Hale, Senator Bingham, and members of the House and Senate Naval Affairs Committees. Britten [Chairman, House Naval Affairs Committee] has already told me that he will do whatever I say. I can cover the House Naval Affairs Committee; Gunnell [Capt. J.H. of BUAER] will cover Mr. French [of House Appropriations]. . . . the thing to do would be for you to talk to Senator Hale, Senator Bingham and other members of hte Senate Naval Affairs Committee that you know well enough to do so. . . . A word from you to any of these people would carry much weight and influence. . . . Fulton [Cdr. Garland, head of Lighter-than-Air in BUAER] tells me that he has seen D.W. Taylor [former Chief of Construction and Repair], and that Taylor is to see Bingham and Hale. . . . I am going up to see Vinson myself today.[70]

PATTERNS

Moffett pulled out all the stops. He solicited the support of members of Congress, his followers in BUAER, allies within the Navy, the Chairman of the National Advisory Committee on Aeronautics, aircraft manufacturers, newspaper publishers, and powerful friends such as Wrigley. Moffett orchestrated his campaign carefully. He portrayed himself as committed to the betterment of the Navy, an advocate of aviation in a service which did not always appreciate it, an able and efficient administrator, and an effective lobbyist. He was also circumspect; as he wrote to Land, "support of the industry will have to be delicately handled. . . . I would not ask any of them, myself personally, to do anything."[71]

At the end of January 1929, Moffett made his case to Secretary of the Navy Wilbur:

> Aeronautics is new. . . . Background and continuity of policies and administration count heavily in such a situation.
>
> The Five Year Program has some two years to run. Having had much to do with this program from its inception and especially in its contact with Congress, I regard it as a work half finished. . . . I have experience and background which is possessed by no one else.
>
> . . . I believe that inside of another year there will be a renewed and more determined activity towards a united air service, and . . . I believe that my background and experience and thorough knowledge of the situation will be of great value to the Navy, as it was . . . during the Mitchell controversy.
>
> . . . Aeronautics is regarded critically by a part of the service, due I believe to lack of knowledge and understanding, but still . . . real. I do not wish to leave a position that is under fire or half finished. . . .[72]

Moffett also argued that airship development, carrier construction and the question of how best to recruit, train, and select pilots were incomplete or unresolved and could benefit from his experience. He understood, he said, the sacrifice involved:

> I believe the Bureau of Aeronautics and the Navy Department ought to have the benefit of [my] knowledge and experience. . . . I realize that I am sacrificing the completion of my strictly Naval career and the flying of my flag at sea, for the sake of continuing to sponsor aeronautical development in the Navy . . . my work in connection with Aviation will have resulted in the preventing of my advancement at sea to the higher commands, which ordinarily I would have been justified . . . in aiming for.[73]

This last was an interesting and not implausible argument. Moffett had won the Medal of Honor for his seamanship and bravery at Vera Cruz in 1914. For his administration of Great Lakes Naval Training Station during World War I, he had been awarded the Distinguished Service Medal. There could be no question of his ability as an officer. His flag rank was not a political gift or the product of longevity. His claim that he might have indeed sacrificed higher rank to remain BUAER Chief had to be considered. Moffett wound up his appeal to Wilbur disingenuously:

> I feel sure, from the great number of people who have spontaneously approached me and urged me to remain, that not only the personnel in Aviation in the Navy but that also generally in aeronautical circles there is a great desire to have

AIR LEADERSHIP

> me remain.... I gave the matter most careful consideration before I made up my mind that it might be in the best interests of the service for me to [stay] ... provided most particularly that it met with the approval of the Secretary of the Navy and the President. ...[74]

Even though Wilbur did not stay on as Navy Secretary, Moffett's tactics prevailed. As Moffett wrote to Wrigley after Herbert Hoover's inauguration:

> There was a great battle.... The Chief of Naval Operations and the Chief of Bureau of Navigation, I think, did all that they could with the new Secretary to show him that my reappointment would be a mistake.... I think that your letter to Mr. Hoover was the deciding factor.[75]

But the matter was not finished. Moffett had again to head off an effort to move him out of BUAER in 1929. He did so by writing to his political friends. To Wrigley, he said:

> I find that the people in the Navy who opposed my reappointment ... have been very active in having me go to sea ... some time between now and the spring. Much work has been done to sell this idea to the Secretary of the Navy, Mr. Adams. ... I want to be ready to do all that I can to prevent the consummation of this plot.
>
> ... I do not want you to write or to do anything, unless possibly, if you met the President and could talk to him you might tell him that you were very much gratified at his appointing me, and that he had, in your opinion, made no mistake. ...[76]

From 1930 until he died in the crash of the airship *Akron* in April 1933, Moffett's position was secure. He was given a six-month extension of his position as BUAER Chief in the spring of 1933 so that he could retire (at age 65) in the post that November. During his third term as head of BUAER, *Akron* was completed (September 1931), *Ranger* (the first ship designed specifically as a carrier) was launched, and Navy aviation went to sea. In Fleet Problem IX of 1929, the carriers *Lexington* and *Saratoga* demonstrated the potential of offensive air forces launched from carriers. It was good that they did; both had been fiscal disasters, and Moffett called them "a permanent handicap."[77] In January 1931, Adm. W.V. Pratt, Chief of Naval Operations, and Gen. Douglas MacArthur, the Army's Chief of Staff, signed an agreement which gave the Army Air Corps responsibility for coast defense aviation. The agreement was no defeat for the Navy. Aviation had at last joined the fleet—at sea; true coast defense was the responsibility of the U.S. Fleet and its *mobile* air arm. Moffett's 1921 promise to put aviation to sea was fact.[78]

According to Emory S. Land, BUAER's assistant chief under Moffett, Moffett was basically "an accomplished public relations man."[79] British naval historian Stephen Roskill took a more positive view: "No other single step was to prove as fruitful for the U.S. Navy, and have such far-reaching effects, as [Moffett's] appointment."[80] Was Moffett indeed a good administrator or was publicity his real talent? Anyone who has seen the 1929 movie "Hell Divers" knows Moffett was a master of publicity. He deliberately put Navy aviation before the public and kept it there, despite danger to lives and property. Navy participation in races slacked off only after *Shenandoah* crashed in 1925, as Moffett grew more cautious in his efforts to promote an image of naval aviation as exciting and technically advanced, but he continued to find ways to promote Navy flying, particularly Navy airships.

He was also a master of persuasion and political lobbying. He studied the members of Congress whose impressions and attitudes would influence BUAER budgets and programs, and he shamelessly cultivated their friendship, often impressing them and the public at the same time. The *Akron* and *Macon* were ideal for this sort of combined lobbying and public relations approach, as the following note from Moffett to Carl Vinson in December 1931 shows:

> Upon my return from the flight of the *Akron* over your district, I want to tell you the pleasure it gave me. . . . It was a beautiful morning, and we arrived at a time when the people . . . were able to see the ship. We were particular to circle each place several times and to fly over the schools. . . . the thought occurred to me, as I looked over the country and the cities, that the people were all your friends and how fortunate they are to have you represent them in Congress. . . . I have had the honor and pleasure of knowing you a great many years, and feel that they are to be congratulated. [81]

Sycophancy? Or the necessary and even enjoyable business of cultivating congressional support? How can the two be separated? Moffett well understood the need for money. Without substantial appropriations, there would be no "hidden subsidy" for the aircraft industry, no carriers and airships, insufficient aircraft for training and for sustaining the carrier squadrons, and no support for developing needed innovations such as radial engines. Moffett also understood the need to defeat General Mitchell's campaign for a separate air force. To defeat Mitchell, Moffett knew he needed to ally himself with the Army; he did and the tactic worked. Moffett knew aviation was expensive; he knew it needed protection at a time when military spending as a whole was on the decline; he knew it would be some years before the full potential of aviation would be appreciated. Results would prove themselves in time; Moffett bought time and money.

Moffett must also be given credit for his administration of BUAER. As I have argued, the Navy made a serious, lasting commitment to fleet aviation even before Moffett arrived in Washington. This commitment was sustained by CNOs Coontz (1919–23), Eberle (1923–27), Hughes (1927–30), and Pratt (1930–33). It was supported by Admirals W.S. Sims and Harris Laning, commandants of the Naval War College, through their work with war games. Experience in the annual fleet problems provided solid evidence in favor of aviation at sea, particularly in 1929. So, too, did the bombing trials undertaken by aircraft against the obsolete armored cruiser *Pittsburgh* and destroyers *Marcus* and *Sloat* in 1930.[82]

As Professor I.B. Holley of Duke University has argued, the essence of military professionalism is the commitment to a rational analysis of doctrine through the sifting of evidence.[83] Moffett benefited tremendously from the widespread commitment to this concept of professionalism which existed in the Navy. Officers who did not like aviation but who nevertheless were good professionals had to accept the evidence that aircraft spotting was essential to very long-range daytime gunnery; that carrier aircraft (certainly by 1929) were capable of finding and sinking enemy ships; and that (by the mid-1930s) long-range seaplanes were essential to fleet reconnaissance. There were very serious professional debates among aviators and between aviators and non-aviators in the Navy over the proper design of carriers, over the best means to protect carriers from attack, and over issues such as the value of recruiting all pilots from the ranks of officers.[84] Moffett could and did rely on this shared sense of professionalism. It was Captain Reeves, for example, who showed the aviators on *Langley* that they could more than triple their effective complement. With more aircraft per carrier, each carrier gained the ability to strike directly at the enemy. It was Reeves who made possible an aircraft strike force—not Moffett. Yet Moffett did not take credit for Reeves' accomplishment, or perceive Reeves as a rival or threat.

Moffett knew what he really wanted: to remain Chief of BUAER, and he outmaneuvered all rivals for that post. In 1925, for instance, Moffett feared he would be sent to the General Board and replaced by Captain Gherardi, but it was Gherardi who went to the General Board. In 1929, Moffett believed Admirals Hughes and Leigh were part of a conspiracy to force him aside in favor of Rear Adm. A.W. Marshall, the first captain of the *Lexington* and later Commandant of the Eighth Naval District and BUAER's training base at Pensacola. Moffett held on so tenaciously because he believed his presence was indeed crucial to progress in naval aviation and because he liked the influence, publicity, and connections which he developed and received. His position as BUAER Chief had placed him in circles where he was both comfortable and competent. In the twenties, he corresponded easily with men such as James F.J. Archibald of Paramount Pictures and Russell Owen of the *New York Times*. Moffett enjoyed appearing before Congress, flying in airships, visiting air shows, and making public appearances. In his letters to his patron Wrigley and his subordinate Land, he complained again and again about the personal cost of remaining as BUAER Chief. I suspect these statements of regret were at once both true and contrived. Moffett enjoyed the politics, prestige, and publicity of his post, but he bristled at criticism and tired of controversy. He was under a lot of pressure in the fall and winter of 1928–29 because his critics and opponents had a point: Moffett had become identified with BUAER, and there was the chance that the conflicts generated by him would hurt the organization which he claimed he was supporting and leading.

Moffett was saved from defeat and retirement, however, by more than influential patrons and acquaintances. He was a sound administrator. He took control of an organization with a number of talented members, and he used that talent to the advantage of the organization. He encouraged innovation and experimentation. He decentralized decisionmaking. He had no choice; he was absent much of the time at meetings, speaking engagements, congressional hearings, and publicity events. As Norman Friedman's detailed study of carrier design shows, however, Moffett's subordinates were quite capable of working within the bureau system and of arguing their cases before the General Board.[85] They had Moffett's confidence, and he theirs. Further evidence of mutual trust is the fact that Moffett did not claim leadership as a function of his technical skill. Moffett never claimed to be BUAER's best engineer or best pilot. He did not have to be; his legitimacy had different roots.

When BUAER was created, there were few senior Navy officers who had both the managerial and aviation experience necessary to structure the new organization and sell it to the Navy and Congress. The aviators needed someone who would support them and lead them. Moffett did both. According to Leighton, his most striking quality was loyalty to subordinates.[86] "Admiral Radford maintained," notes historian Charles Melhorn, "that much of U.S. naval aviation's early progress was due to a decision by Admiral Moffett that a flyer was not to be penalized for an honest mistake."[87] Moffett also kept the right face to the right audience. To the public, Navy aviation was daring and its pilots dashing; to the fleet, Navy aviation was professional and its standards exacting.

As a developing organization subject to changes in a new and developing technology, BUAER needed:

1. Management which appreciated technical problems and knew how to generate the "hidden subsidies" required to solve them.

2. Leadership willing to finance multiple approaches to the same problem until a clear solution was in sight. Moffett favored airships over seaplanes for long-range scouting, but he did not curtail seaplane development because of his beliefs.

3. Management aware of the inevitability of "wastage" in a new technology and ready to pay for it.

AIR LEADERSHIP

4. Leadership which understood the need to develop and then continually revise aviation doctrine in light of simulations and exercises.
5. The means to move pilots into senior commands so that younger men could look forward to substantial Navy careers.

Moffett comprehended the importance of these needs and satisfied (not always successfully) each. He was not without his flaws. As an administrator, he played favorites and had difficulty working with younger men who did not like him personally. As BUAER Chief, he misused the airships for publicity purposes. He was also criticized for allowing severe cost overruns on the conversion of the battle cruisers *Lexington* and *Saratoga* to carriers. He supported the small carrier (*Ranger*) against larger designs (*Yorktown*) which proved more effective, and he was an advocate of the hybrid carrier-cruiser.[88] By 1930 Moffett had significant control over the policies—not just the administration—of BUAER, and I believe the consequences were less than positive for Navy aviation.

Rear Adm. W. A. Moffett was a complex man. Ambitious, proud, energetic, brave, and intensely (sometimes blindingly) patriotic, he fostered the finest naval aviation organization in the world. However, he did not give the Navy its wings, nor did he ever claim to have done so. In many ways he compares with Adm. H.G. Rickover. Both men, certainly, were "bureaucratic entrepreneurs."[89] Both realized their ambitions and built their influence from staff positions in the Navy's central administration. Both could be consummate politicians in budget battles; both understood how to generate favorable publicity and how to cultivate powerful images for the organizations they headed.

But the similarity ends there. Moffett could and did claim respect for his accomplishments as a seagoing and combat commander. Rickover could not. Unlike Rickover, Moffett did not have to train a corps of specialists to develop a new technology. He had them; his job was to support them and give them the tools necessary to make aviation an essential element of the U.S. Fleet. Moffett was less bureaucrat than politician; he enjoyed the art of persuasion and the company of the influential. He knew he and naval aviation needed allies, and he got them; because the Army also had a claim to aviation, he had to take a broader view than Admiral Rickover. Moffett dared not ignore the Army or wage political war against Army aviation, and that need to reach across service boundaries restrained his rhetoric and his influence. Unlike General Mitchell, Moffett would never become a popular martyr for aviation. Unlike Rickover, he could never ignore the other services.[90]

New military technologies and the bureaucracies which foster them require a political style of leadership, because their promise is at first only that—a potential without concrete evidence of its value. The danger is that administrative leadership which is too politically effective and too clever will promise more in a technical sense than it can deliver, or will deliver the wrong stuff. Yet "political" leadership there must be, or the new technology will not develop. The need for this "political" leadership places strains on the people and on the formal and informal rules which constitute the immediate reality of a military bureaucracy.

For a military officer, shifting from a traditional role to a "political" one means abandoning a secure basis of legitimacy for one which his colleagues may not respect. It means—professionally and morally—going out on a limb. It is a tactic which must be employed if military organizations are to ride the crest of the wave of technology, but it is not a tactic many military officers can use skillfully. Indeed, we would not want many who could. Otherwise, we might find more admirals like Rickover in Navy billets meant for captains. However, managers and leaders like Moffett are essential—if risky—whenever a new military technology is introduced at the expense of existing weapons or programs.

In his detailed study of the Polaris Missile submarine project, Harvey Sapolsky argued that it "succeeded because its proponents possessed admirable quantities of political and technological skill and were the beneficiaries of good fortune."[91] My point is that Moffett and BUAER succeeded for the same reasons. Indeed, the essence of peacetime military leadership in a time of rapid technological change is political (both partisan and bureaucratic) acumen coupled with the necessary "good fortune"—not special, apolitical managerial techniques.

Notes

1. Research for this paper was supported by a contract from the Office of Net Assessment, Department of Defense, and by a grant from the Earhart Foundation of Ann Arbor, Michigan. Dr. Wayne Thompson and Dr. Mark D. Mandeles strongly aided and encouraged me in this work. Lt George H. Moffett, USN, Retired, gave me permission to use his father's correspondence.

2. *United States Naval Aviation, 1910–1970*, Naval Air Systems Command (Washington, 1970), NAVAIR 00–80P–1, p 9.

3. *Ibid*, p 35.

4. "U.S. Naval Administration in World War II: BUAER," typewritten manuscript, US Navy Library, Washington Navy Yard, I, 34–35.

5. W. A. Moffett to William Wrigley, Jr., 14 Nov 1924, Moffett papers, U.S. Naval Academy Library.

6. Moffett to Wrigley, 29 Jul 1921, Moffett papers.

7. Moffett had also been Vice President of the Army-Navy Club of Chicago, and he was even active in the Izaak Walton League. Wrigley had also introduced Moffett to Ogden Armour of the meat packing family. Moffett to Wrigley, 12 Nov 1924, Moffett papers.

8. Moffett to Wrigley, 14 Nov 1924, Moffett papers.

9. "U.S. Naval Administration in World War II: BUAER," I, 45.

10. W.R. Braisted, "Charles Frederick Hughes," in *The Chiefs of Naval Operations*, ed by R.W. Love (Annapolis, 1980), p 60.

11. "U.S. Naval Administration in World War II: BUAER," I, 38.

12. See Thomas Hone and Norman Friedman, "Innovation and Administration in the Navy Department: The Case of the *Nevada* Design," *Military Affairs*, Apr 81.

13. "Hearings before the General Board of the U.S. Navy" (hereafter referred to as "Hearings"), 18 Jan 1919, p 1. See also "Hearings," 12 May 1919, pp 18–19, and 17 Apr 1919, p 14. The stenographic records of the hearings and the General Board studies are held by the Classified Operational Archives of the U.S. Navy.

14. "Hearings," 10 Mar 1919, p 234.

15. "Hearings," 27 Mar 1919, p 371.

16. "Hearings," 6 May 1919, p 864.

17. "Hearings," 9 Jun 1919, p 890.

18. "Hearings," 5 Mar 1919, p 177.

19. "Hearings," 12 May 1919, p 935.

20. "Hearings," 25 Apr 1919, pp 800–01.

21. Memo from General Board to Secretary of Navy, "Future Policy Governing Development of Air Service for the United States Navy," G.B. No. 449, Serial #887, 23 Jun 1919.

22. "Hearings," 6 May 1919, p 884.

23. Charles Melhorn, *Two-Block Fox: The Rise of the Aircraft Carrier, 1911–1929* (Annapolis, 1974), pp 154–55, note 34.

24. Clifford Lord, "The History of Naval Aviation, 1898–1939," unpublished manuscript, Naval Aviation History Unit, Office of the Deputy Chief of Naval Operations (Air), 1946, in the Navy Department Library, Washington Navy Yard, Part III, p 834.

25. Hone and Friedman, "Innovation and Administration in the Navy Department."

26. "Hearings," 1 Nov 1920, p 923.

27. *United States Naval Aviation, 1910–1970*, p 48.

28. *Ibid*.

AIR LEADERSHIP

29. Lord, "The History of Naval Aviation, 1898–1939," Part III, p 841.
30. *United States Naval Aviation, 1910–1970*, p 48.
31. Lord, "The History of Naval Aviation, 1898–1939," Part III, p 838.
32. Moffett to W.S. Sims, 28 Feb 1922, Moffett papers.
33. Melhorn, *Two-Block Fox*, p 152, note 9.
34. Mitchell had already tried to block Moffett's appointment as BUAER Chief, but his effort had been rejected by the Joint Board of the Army and Navy. See Melhorn, *Two-Block Fox*, pp 69–73. For an excellent discussion of Mitchell's methods and ideas, see A. F. Hurley, *Billy Mitchell: Crusader for Air Power* (New York, 1964).
35. Melhorn, *Two-Block Fox*, pp 154–155, note 34. Also see T. Hone, "Spending Patterns of the U.S. Navy, 1921–1941," *Armed Forces and Society*, Spring 1982. Hurley, in *Billy Mitchell*, chapters 4 and 6, considered the flaws in Mitchell's position.
36. "Hearings," 7 Jul 1922, p 581.
37. *Ibid*, p 578.
38. D. H. Robinson and C. L. Keller, *Up Ship: A History of the U.S. Navy's Rigid Airships, 1919–1935* (Annapolis, 1982), pp 58–59.
39. Quoted by R. F. Futrell, *Ideas, Concepts, Doctrine: A History of Basic Thinking in the United States Air Force, 1907–1964* (Maxwell AFB, Ala., 1971), p 26.
40. Quoted by R.W. Turk, "Edward Walter Eberle," in Love, ed., *The Chiefs of Naval Operations*, p 41.
41. *United States Naval Aviation, 1910–1970*, p 57. See also Stephen Roskill, *Naval Policy Between the Wars, Vol I* (New York, 1968), p 399.
42. Roskill, *Naval Policy Between the Wars, Vol I*, p 467.
43. Memo from Chief BUAER to Secretary of Navy via the CNO, "Naval Aeronautic Policy," 10 Aug 1922, Moffett papers, paragraph 1.
44. *Ibid*, paragraph 4.
45. *Ibid*, paragraph 5.
46. *Ibid*, paragraph 7.
47. The phrase is I. B. Holley's. See his *Buying Aircraft: Materiel Procurement for the Army Air Forces*, United States Army in World War II, Special Studies (Washington, 1964).
48. Quoted by Futrell, *Ideas, Concepts, Doctrine*, p 26.
49. *United States Naval Aviation, 1910–1970*, p 58. See also Futrell, *Ideas, Concepts, Doctrine*, pp 26–27; Roskill, *Naval Policy Between the Wars*, Vol I, p 468. Mitchell had no allies in the group which offered technical support to the Morrow Board. Moffett had two of his proteges in that group: Cdrs. Jerome Hunsaker and H.C. Richardson. See Hurley, *Billy Mitchell*, p 102; Gerald Wheeler, "Mitchell, Moffett, and Air Power," *The Airpower Historian*, Vol VIII, No 2 (Apr 1961), 79–87.
50. Futrell, *Ideas, Concepts, Doctrine*, p 28.
51. Roskill, *Naval Policy Between the Wars, Vol I*, p 469; *United States Naval Aviation, 1910–1970*, p 59.
52. Clifford L. Lord, "The History of Naval Aviation, 1898–1939," Part IV, pp 1178–81.
53. Melhorn, *Two-Block Fox*, p 113.
54. Geoffrey Till, *Air Power in the Royal Navy, 1914–1945* (London, 1979), p 72.
55. Letter from Rear Adm. J. M. Reeves, Commander Aircraft Squadrons Battle Fleet, to Moffett, 4 Oct 1928, Moffett papers.
56. Moffett to Wrigley, 12 Nov 1924, Moffett papers.
57. Moffett to Wrigley, 11 Feb 1925, Moffett papers.
58. Robinson and Keller, *Up Ship: A History of the U.S. Navy's Rigid Airships, 1919–1935*, p 71.
59. *Ibid*, pp 77–91.
60. There are records of two lectures: (1) "Light Aircraft Carriers, Comparison with Light Cruisers as Fleet Units," May 1927; (2) "The Relation Between Air and Surface Activities in the Navy," Mar 1928. See *Naval Aviation History*, Naval Air Systems Command, pp 43–55.
61. Melhorn, *Two-Block Fox*, p 118, note 5.
62. Admiral Pride's remark is in "For the Good of the Ship," a sketch of Moffett's career

by his son, Rear Adm. W. A. Moffett, Jr., in *Foundation*, Naval Aviation Museum, Vol 4, No 2, Fall 1983, p 40.

63. Braisted, "Charles Frederick Hughes," pp 49–68.

64. *Akron* cost $5,375,000; *Macon* was far more reasonable at $2,450,000, because of lessons learned with *Akron*. However, *Akron* logged only 1,696 hours over 73 flights before crashing. *Macon* flew 1,798 hours on 54 flights. Carrier *Ranger* had cost $12.5 million to build. Newer heavy cruisers cost about $8 million to build and another $3 million to arm and equip; their service life was officially 20 years. See *Naval Expenditures, 1933* (Washington, 1934), p 275. See also Cdr. Garland Fulton, *Transactions of the Society of Naval Architects and Marine Engineers*, "Some Features of a Modern Airship—U.S.S. *Akron*," Vol 39, 1931, pp 135–154.

65. Memo, from Chief BUAER to Secretary of Navy, 23 Jan 1928, "Reasons why duties assigned Bureau of Aeronautics in General Order 65, Art. 7(a) should not be removed by the Secretary of the Navy," Moffett papers.

66. Memo from Moffett to Secretary of Navy, "Naval Aviation Personnel Policy," 21 Sep 1925, Moffett papers.

67. Lord, "The History of Naval Aviation, 1898–1939," Part IV, p 1169.

68. Moffett to Wrigley, 7 May 1928, Moffett papers.

69. Moffett to Wrigley, 13 Oct 1928, Moffett papers.

70. Moffett to E. S. Land, 17 Dec 1928, Moffett papers.

71. *Ibid*.

72. Moffett to Secretary of Navy, 21 Jan 1929, Moffett papers.

73. *Ibid*.

74. *Ibid*.

75. Moffett to Wrigley, 13 Mar 1929, Moffett papers.

76. Moffett to Wrigley, 26 Nov 1929, Moffett papers.

77. Moffett's comments to the General Board are cited in Roskill, *Naval Policy Between the Wars, Vol I*, p 470. Records covering Fleet Problem IX are in National Archives publication M964, which covers the Confidential Correspondence of Secretary of Navy, File A16-3.

78. In his report for 1929, the Secretary of the Navy summarized the distribution of fleet aviation this way: 15 squadrons with the battle fleet, 5 with the scouting fleet, 2 with the Asiatic fleet, one squadron on a survey mission, and most of the remaining assigned aircraft (71 of a total of 116) at Pensacola. *Annual Report of the Secretary of the Navy, 1929*, pp 597–598. See also *Navy Directory*, 1 Apr 1929, Navy Dept., Bureau of Navigation, Chap. 5.

79. Melhorn, *Two-Block Fox*, p 142.

80. Roskill, *Naval Policy Between the Wars, Vol I*, pp 249–50.

81. Moffett to Carl Vinson, 23 Dec 1931, Moffett papers.

82. Lord, "The History of Naval Aviation, 1898–1939," Part IV, p 1211.

83. I. B. Holley, "Of Saber Charges, Escort Fighters, and Spacecraft," *Air University Review*, XXXIV, No 6, (1983), 2–11.

84. T. Hone and M. Mandeles, "Managerial Style in the Interwar Navy: A Reappraisal," *Naval War College Review*, Sep-Oct 1980.

85. Norman Friedman, *U.S. Aircraft Carriers, An Illustrated Design History* (Annapolis, 1983).

86. Eugene E. Wilson, *Slipstream* (New York, 1950), p 20.

87. Melhorn, *Two-Block Fox*, p 146, note 21.

88. "Hearings," 4 and 5 Dec 1930, 23 Dec 1930, 16 and 17 Jul 1931.

89. Eugene Lewis, *Public Entrepreneurship: Toward a Theory of Bureaucratic Political Power* (Bloomington, Indiana, 1980).

90. Adm Rickover's career is described in R. G. Hewlett and F. Duncan, *Nuclear Navy* (Chicago, 1974).

91. Harvey Sapolsky, *The Polaris System Development* (Cambridge, 1972), p 183.

Air Force Leadership and Business Methods: Some Suggestions for Biographers

Harry R. Borowski

Our fascination with biographies stems largely from an interest in the human qualities we admire and can develop within ourselves. The most gripping works describe how individuals have overcome great odds by strength of character. We entertain to varying degrees a Great Man theory: Napoleon built an empire and Bismarck unified a nation. Biographers have focused on personal traits and often explained success or failure in those terms.

Without deprecating the accomplishments of past leaders, one can argue that it is more difficult today for a single person to emerge as a driving force behind great events. Societies have spawned bureaucracies in response to increasing complexity in all areas of life. The ability to work within this growing maze of man-made constraints and achieve traditional objectives marks the successful leader. For military commanders, this ability has been particularly important since 1940.

Historians recognize that the Allies defeated the Axis in a total conflict where all elements of society contributed to the war effort. While combat commanders helped to make victory possible, total war demanded a host of activities at home which required managerial skills and expertise—often provided by business and industry. For integrating these activities few men were decorated, but their contribution was absolutely necessary in a war where the crucial factor became which side could out-produce the other and bring that production to bear on the battlefield. The emphasis on combat and personal leadership in military biography has served a useful purpose in motivating and training young men entering the armed forces. That emphasis, however, may also have distorted our understanding of the total effort.

I do not wish to set up a straw man. Excellent biographies have addressed the managerial skills of military leaders—Forrest Pogue's outstanding study of George C. Marshall being a prime example.[1] But works of this nature have appeared infrequently, and in recent years hardly at all. One possible reason comes to mind.

AIR LEADERSHIP

The Vietnam War greatly influenced the way military men thought about leadership and management. Officers and civilians alike probed every dimension of that war, seeking possible answers that would explain our unhappy experience. Leadership, from presidents down to company commanders, became a popular focus of discussion. Gabriel and Savage's *Crisis in Command* did much to launch us on a questionable path.[2] Much of the war's failure, the authors argued, resulted from poor leadership; commanders did not lead their men but tried to manage their troops. To many officers the lesson was obvious: soldiers risking their lives for their country needed a leader not a manager. For those trying to determine what went wrong in Vietnam, this simplistic explanation held obvious attraction. If the services once again stressed traditional military values or leadership, and others (civilians) handled management tasks, we would do better in the future. Very soon, leadership took on the status of virtue; management the antithesis. Somehow the two were not to be found in the same person.

This new concept gained popularity with officers and defense watchers, including the so-called military reform group (which also holds that there is too much emphasis on high technology and attrition of enemy forces). Military journals printed frequent articles addressing the dichotomy, and more than one major paper at an intermediate service school zeroed in on this "new discovery." The whole argument grew out of proportion, despite the pleas of management-trained officers. Recently however, *Air University Review* and *Military Affairs* have published articles treating leadership and management with more balance.[3] If we want future biographies to be as useful as possible, the management dimension of our military leaders must not be ignored in favor of their personalities. The management dimension can be more important to the outcome of a conflict in today's complex world.

In addition to Vietnam, there are other reasons why biographers have avoided the management dimension. To analyze management requires close examination of an organization, its decisionmaking processes, and the interaction between its parts and other organizations. Not only is such an effort formidable, but there is often insufficient evidence to support strong conclusions. Until these dimensions are better understood, individual roles cannot be accurately appreciated.

President Eisenhower spoke cautiously of a growing military industrial complex. Writers with a bent for conspiracy theory found his warning ominous. Critics of the military have long delighted in showing a close relationship (collusion by implication) between the Pentagon and corporate America. Perhaps this is our legacy from the 1930s, when Senator Gerald Nye led an investigation of business's role in the First World War. For whatever reason, biographers of military leaders often shy away from fully addressing important relationships between those leaders and business.

If you ponder this attitude, it should trouble you. Our society, with its particular mix of free enterprise and representative government, has produced outstanding armies with superior equipment and technology—certainly nothing of which to be ashamed. Our powerful military did not simply happen. In the post-World War II period, we find close cooperation between industry and the services to achieve this end. How our military leaders functioned in the complex world of congressional committees, staffers, lobbies, and business to develop a viable military force should be of utmost interest to biographers.

Several business historians have demonstrated the value of looking at management skills. In 1947 the husband and wife team of Ralph and Muriel Hidy obtained permission from Standard Oil of New Jersey to research company archives and write a history of the company from formation to dissolution by the Supreme Court in 1911.[4] As professional scholars rather than modern-day muckrakers, the Hidys wanted to understand corporate leadership, its decisionmaking process, and the rise of Standard Oil. Their history did not totally please Standard Oil but put to rest certain misperceptions about the early corporation. Success came not from "robber baron" operations, the Hidys concluded, but from a combination of business acumen and logical responses to new economic, political, and legal forces. John D. Rockefeller and his lieutenants recognized the changes underway in America, and through vision and better accounting, they planned more effectively than their competitors. Modern-day muckrakers found little in the volume that interested them, but the Hidys had made a giant leap in our understanding of how American business developed during this dynamic period. It was, in short, a combination of leadership and management skills working together that brought Standard Oil its success.[5]

After the Hidys completed their impressive volume, Alfred D. Chandler, Jr., began a similar study of four U.S. business giants between 1890 and 1921—a period including the unsettling impact of World War I.[6] Focusing on four corporations (the reorganized Standard Oil, Du Pont, General Motors, and Sears and Roebuck), he determined that chief executives in each corporation perceived important changes underway in the American economy and successfully developed strategies to succeed within that new environment. The corporations then restructured their organizations to support their new strategies. Once centralized management determined strategy, execution fell to a decentralized structure of functional divisions—marketing, finance, and so forth. The pattern continued when each corporation chose to diversify. Chandler's story was biographical in the sense

AIR LEADERSHIP

that he showed the impact of personalities in each company. At the same time, he demonstrated that changes within the American economic and political scene required adaptations on the part of business. Successful business leaders understood and responded with a rare combination of management acumen, personal leadership, and entrepreneurship.

I do not hold that a biographical treatment stressing management skills would be ideal for a World War I leader like Gen. John J. Pershing. I do wonder, however, if such an approach might be needed when writing military biography for World War II commanders. For like the Rockefellers and the Du Ponts, Gen. Henry H. "Hap" Arnold and Adm. Chester W. Nimitz found themselves operating in an environment quite different from that which they had experienced a decade earlier. Management became a more important dimension of leadership. How they were able to succeed in this new environment is of the greatest interest.

Much of the business history written before World War II came out of the progressive or robber baron tradition; scholars tended to judge industry leaders on the basis of moral issues and put capitalism on trial. The tradition continues today among those scholars who see the military-industrial complex as a negative force in the American economy. During the 1950s, however, a number of works appeared that were less concerned about such value judgments and more interested in the way corporations made their decisions and why they succeeded. In the new histories written by the Hidys and Chandler, among others, institutional needs for continued success overshadowed the personal characteristics of company directors. This relationship may partially explain why fewer biographies have been written of businessmen living past the early 1930s.

The same reality may be present in military history, albeit to a much lesser degree. America's most recent and longest conflict, the Vietnam War, has stimulated few biographies. What has proven most successful and valuable instead are works analyzing America's institutional decisionmaking process and its strategy for conducting operations.[7] Military personalities do not come to the fore, Gen. William C. Westmoreland notwithstanding.

Interestingly enough, after Chandler completed his volume on strategy and structure, he agreed to edit the papers of Dwight D. Eisenhower. Chandler soon found evidence suggesting striking parallels between Ike's command experiences during World War II and that of corporate leaders after World War I. Eisenhower's success, Chandler argued, came from his ability (with the support of Gen. George C. Marshall) to create a command organization which could defeat the Axis forces. The key consideration was unity of command. Ike retained overall control of strategy, but he gave his commanders the resources and flexibility to do their jobs. It was again centralized planning but decentralized execution. "In modern war, as in modern business, strategic planning has become a staff agency."[8] Though Chandler was quick to point out that Ike never forgot the basics of keeping an army up for fighting, Chandler had more admiration for the general's ability to work with governments, individuals, and agencies (many competing with each other) and to put them in harness together. Chandler found many similar leadership and management qualities in Ike, Alfred P. Sloan, Jr., of General Motors, and Robert E. Wood of Sears and Roebuck.

More recently, William P. Snyder wrote an excellent piece for *Military Affairs* on Lt. Gen. Walter Bedell Smith's performance as Eisenhower's chief of staff. Certainly not as well known as Gen. Omar N. Bradley or Field Marshal Bernard L. Montgomery, Smith's role was no less crucial as the "general manager" of the war, to use Ike's own words.[9] Clearly Smith stood at the head of the class; certain postwar generals, however, needed remedial work after school, and they failed because they lacked management skills. For example, Maj. Gen. Clements McMullen, Deputy Commander of Strategic Air Command (SAC) under Gen. George C. Kenney, held staff officers in contempt. Effective command of SAC fell to him under Kenney's tenure, and he quickly abolished a number of staff positions and activities or assumed their functions himself.[10] Had he been able to run SAC as commander and staff all rolled into one, we would need biographies on his outstanding leadership! McMullen's failure, however, demonstrated an inability to adapt to changes brought about by World War II; his prewar experience worked to his detriment in the same way that business leaders like Henry Ford had been unable to adapt after World War I.

Consequently, the way in which successful air leaders modified force structure after World War II is most deserving of our attention. Over the past thirty years, the military has often been accused of trying too hard to emulate corporate organization, and perhaps the charge has some validity. In the 1950s, many aspiring officers wanted to attend the Harvard Business School, and Air Force uniforms began to look more like business suits than traditional military garb. But one could argue that postwar air leaders were just trying to amalgamate the best of the business world with traditional military concepts of organization. Biographers might find this a fertile field for research. Several examples come to mind.

Within two months of the war's end, the Assistant Secretary of War for Air, Robert A. Lovett, urged General Arnold to improve the management techniques of the Army Air Forces (AAF).[11] Demobilization called for special efforts along these lines. "During the war one of the outstanding accomplishments of the Army Air Forces Staff," Lovett argued, "was the adaption of certain basic business principles to military needs and the handling of problems that are essentially those of a business enterprise."[12] Given future constraints, the AAF would have to become even more efficient in its use of resources, and a special internal agency structured to ensure such efficiency would help execute postwar strategies. The AAF needed, he continued, "to develop an organized, completely coordinated and budgeted program." He wanted to develop

> a unit which embraces a thorough knowledge of the facts from a practical, analytical, and not a bookkeeping angle, of all Air Force components—personnel, material, facilities, expenditures, operations and, with increasing importance, research activities. The most effective solution lies in recognition of the fact that the Air Force is a business enterprise.[13]

John D. Rockefeller, not known for admiring things military, would have applauded this view.

Lovett's solution was to create a simple staff agency with analytical expertise and place it under a senior officer working directly for the Commanding General or his Chief of Staff. To do this, he wanted to centralize the functions of the Office of Program Monitoring, the Office of Statistical Control, and the Budget and Fiscal Office, or to establish them as divisions under a new Air Comptroller General. Not only would economic savings accrue from this structure, but better information for high-level planning and strategy would emerge. The key would be to select a gifted senior officer to direct the new office—someone with good judgement, varied experience, and the ability to render dispassionate advice. In the world of business, the profit and loss statement set the standard for decisionmaking; in the military, an officer would be needed with an appreciation for cost effectiveness and a distaste for advocacy. "The Air Forces have led the other services in progressive business-like practices. I should like to see this record continued in the future," Lovett concluded.[14]

Lovett's idea enjoyed a warm reception from Arnold. Continuing Lovett's arguments, Arnold reminded his key deputies that "the Air Forces in many ways is like a large business institution and we must continue to take advantage of new methods and procedures developed by the business world."[15] He directed his staff to develop plans for implementing this concept within five weeks! The Air Staff concurred with Lovett's recommendation and planning moved quickly.[16]

In February 1946 the new AAF Commanding General, Carl Spaatz, designated Maj. Gen. St. Clair Street to head the comptroller office.[17] Street held the primary responsibility of providing Spaatz "the same kind of advice and technical assistance in his exercise of command that the chief executive of a large business organization has available. . . . In the Army Air Forces *the command function is the management function.*"[18] The Air Comptroller was not to make policy or fulfill command functions, but to give advice and assistance to the Commanding General. The Air Staff remained intact, but a more specialized office now emerged to provide the exacting information and guidance demanded by the postwar period. The legacy of this office and its demand for managerial skills remains with the Air Force today.

The relationship between air leaders and the aviation industry after World War II also warrants examination, and I believe some helpful observations would emerge from such an effort.

We know much about how the government tried to stimulate production of aircraft needed for the war. We know less about the postwar period when declining demand forced many firms to consolidate or go out of business. Air leaders keenly appreciated the problem confronting aircraft corporations; they also knew full well that the industry had to be sustained both to keep the air force modernized and to be ready for another rapid spurt of production if war came again. The Aircraft Industries Association of America (AIA), for example, represented a group of aviation contractors with which the AAF wished to maintain close but proper contact. In fact, two representatives from this group were invited to observe atomic tests BAKER and ABLE.[19] Few if any industries suffered greater problems after World War II than did aircraft manufacturers; members of the AIA tried to predict demand and to plan their companies' activities accordingly.

Concerned about loss of contact with the aviation industry, the Deputy Chief of Staff, Lt. Gen. Ira C. Eaker, wrote the president of the AIA, LaMont Cohu, advising him that the AAF wished:

> to keep in close contact with the element of American industrial life which these manufactures represent. . . . they should be advised of Army Air Forces organization and policies, of changing procurement policies and procedures, and of the ever-developing concept of Air Power.[20]

Maj. Gen. Lauris Norstad, Deputy Chief of Staff for Operations, supported Eaker's view, though Norstad suggested that Eaker's first draft be toned down. Norstad did not wish to give the AAF the appearance of "advocating a propaganda organization" within the AIA.[21] But the need for industry support could not be ignored.

Meanwhile, AIA directors were trying to organize a conference with military and government leaders to discuss future aircraft requirements for national defense. They invited key military leaders, including Maj. Gen. Curtis E. LeMay, the newly named Assistant Chief of Staff for Research and Development. LeMay faced a difficult task. There remained many serious questions about national defense and force structure. When the conference met at Williamsburg, Virginia, in late July 1946, the effects of demobilization were just beginning to appear. LeMay told the group that the AAF considered a new long range bomber like the B–36 its top priority, but he also spoke of new fighters—some that could be carried by bombers, others capable of breaking the speed of sound—as well as reconnaissance planes, troop transports, trainers, rockets, and guided missile systems. Jet propulsion, LeMay stressed, would be the major propulsion system of the future, but he also spoke of using nuclear energy for propulsion. The AAF would help fund research, but industry must be willing to cooperate fully. LeMay's off-the-record speech gave company presidents facts and figures on the direction of AAF procurement in the coming years, and practical suggestions for staying in business. In turn, government leaders learned more about the problems industry faced during those trying times, and what AIA members needed before they could meet future challenges.[22]

The Williamsburg conference illustrated the kind of cooperation necessary in a free market society if a flexible yet cost effective defense structure was to be maintained. The meeting enjoyed no official sanction; in fact had it not been for the good feeling remaining from victory in World War II, this conference might well have been viewed by many as an improper activity of an emerging military-industrial complex. LeMay was joined on the program by twenty high ranking air force leaders including Generals Otto P. Weyland, Laurence C. Craigie, Edward M. Powers, and Nathan F. Twining; Spaatz and Eaker also attended, along with counterparts from the Navy. Certainly the conference was needed—aircraft production had fallen off dramatically after World War II, and since 1944 the AIA had been unsuccessful in trying to secure a congressional policy on readjustment. The companies needed information with which to plan. National requirements would demand "close teamwork of government leaders and aircraft company management."[23]

The aviation industry faced difficult adjustments in the late 1940s, but consolidations and diversification put aircraft companies on a sound footing. No one can claim this relatively stable condition stemmed from leadership by Air Force officials, but their cooperation and sharing of projected demands probably helped firms plan correctly for the future. Unfortunately, when we have heard about interaction between the Air Force and industry, the stories have usually been negative: for example, the deathbed claim by Jack Northrop that the Secretary of the Air Force, Stuart Symington, tried to force a merger of Northrop's firm with Consolidated-Vultee Aircraft Corporation in the late 1940s. That charge seems to have been discredited, but not before it became the focus of a public television special in Los Angeles. At any rate, the memory lingers.[24]

These examples and issues suggest to me that biographers of airpower leaders might do well to examine more carefully several new dimensions. Without ignoring personalities, which have traditionally formed the basis for biography, we need to consider how well leaders have operated in an increasingly complex world of changing economic and political institutions. We would be foolish to overlook management skills, and it would be instructive to compare Air Force organizational structure with that of contemporary industry. Such examinations will be far more difficult to write and probably less enjoyable to read. But they will best continue biography's important role in advancing our knowledge of military affairs.

Notes

1. Forrest C. Pogue, *George C. Marshall: Organizer of Victory* (New York, 1973).
2. Richard A. Gabriel and Paul L. Savage, *Crisis in Command* (New York, 1978).
3. Maj James McDermott, "Leadership and Management: A Balanced Model of Officership," *Air University Review*, Sep 1983, pp 55–63. See also Lt Col Boyd M. Harris, "A Perspective on Leadership, Management, and Command," *Military Review*, Feb 1984, pp 48–57.
4. Ralph W. Hidy and Muriel E. Hidy, *Pioneering in Big Business, 1882–1911* (New York, 1955).
5. *Ibid*, p 25.
6. Alfred D. Chandler, Jr., *Strategy and Structure: Chapters in the History of the Industrial Enterprise* (Cambridge, Mass. 1962).
7. Two excellent works addressing this dimension are George C. Herring, *America's Longest War: The United States and Vietnam, 1950–1975* (New York, 1979), and Leslie H. Gelb with Richard K. Betts, *The Irony of Vietnam: The System Worked* (Washington, 1979).
8. Chandler, ed, *The Papers of Dwight David Eisenhower: The War Years* (Baltimore, 1970), I, xxv.
9. William P. Snyder, "Walter Bedell Smith: Eisenhower's Chief of Staff," *Military Affairs*, Jan 1984, pp 6–14.
10. Harry R. Borowski, *A Hollow Threat* (Westport, Conn. 1982), pp 54–68.
11. Memo, Robert A. Lovett to Gen Henry H. Arnold, subj: Need for Improved and Increased Management Procedures, 5 Oct 1945, LeMay Collection, 168.64-4, Air Force Historical Research Center, Maxwell AFB, Ala. (hereafter cited as AFHRC).
12. *Ibid.*
13. *Ibid.*
14. *Ibid.*
15. Memo for Air Staff, subj: Business Management Procedures in the Air Forces, 24 Oct 1945, LeMay Collection, 168.64-4, AFHRC.
16. Ltr, Gen Lauris Norstad to Deputy Commander AAF, 26 Oct 1945, LeMay Collection, 168.64-4, AFHRC.
17. Ltr, Lt Gen Ira Eaker to Generals Chauncey, LeMay, Anderson, and Col Sims, subj: Proposed Office of Air Comptroller, 19 Feb 1946, LeMay Collection, 168.64-4, AFHRC.
18. Memo to Deputy Commander AAF from Special Consultant to the Commanding General, Edmund P. Learned, Tab A, 26 Jan 1946, LeMay Collection, 168.64-6, AFHRC. General Eaker sent this memo and attachments to General Streett as guidance for his new assignment.
19. Ltr, Maj Gen Curtis LeMay to John E. P. Morgan, Executive Director, AIA, 6 Aug 1946, LeMay Collection, 168.64-6, AFHRC.
20. Ltr, Lt Gen Ira C. Eaker to LaMont Cohu, President AIA, 9 Apr 1946, LeMay Collection, 168.64-6, AFHRC.
21. Memo, Maj Gen Lauris Norstad to Lt Gen Ira Eaker, 6 Apr 1946, LeMay Collection, 168.64-6, AFHRC.
22. See text of speech, "Comments to be Delivered at Aircraft Industries Association at Williamsburg, July 31, 1946," LeMay Collection, 168.64-6, AFHRC.
23. Atch to ltr, John E. P. Morgan to Maj Gen Curtis LeMay, 13 Jun 1946, LeMay Collection, 168.64-6, AFHRC.
24. The Northrop charge has been effectively refuted by Francis J. Baker, "The Death of the Flying Wing: The Real Reasons Behind the 1949 Cancellation of Northrop Aircraft's RB–49," PhD Diss, Claremont Graduate School, 1984.

Comment

Allan R. Millett

It is appropriate to have a meeting like this at what was once Bolling Field and near the Anacostia Naval Air Station—the early homes of what became the Air Force and naval aviation. In fact we are in one of the fortified camps of the many interwar, interservice battles of the Potomac.

Colonel Borowski has given us a fine paper developing the conceptual problems related to the nature of military biography, particularly those of military officers whose major career achievements occur in peacetime. He has quite properly indicated that one of the major challenges of the biographer is to reveal the personality of its subject, that often the study of a personality can then be used to explain events. Colonel Borowski doubts that a single person can be a driving force in peacetime military events, hence the challenge to the biographer of a peacetime military officer. I tend to agree with him. But if the study of the individual is used to examine the history of an institution, we can learn a great deal about both the individual and the organization.

I think Colonel Borowski is quite correct in saying that one needs to understand organization, particularly the peculiarities of an organization, to do a successful peacetime biography. I would suggest, as I have in other forums, that one needs to know at least a little about the theoretical literature on organizational behavior. Organizations are obviously not static in their needs, and the challenges to their leaders may vary over time. For example, most organizations require strong leadership and demand strong leadership in periods of crisis. It is also useful to examine the needs of organizational leaders. The people, particularly in peacetime, who have had the greatest impact upon their services are those who have had time, a great deal of power, and a substantial amount of vision. I don't think it is accidental that in the history of the United States Air Force, for example, people like Hap Arnold and Curtis LeMay stand out as strong leaders, because each had all three of those ingredients.

Mature, stable organizations seem to demand less dramatic leadership. In fact a sign of their maturity is that they do not depend upon one individual. Perhaps the best thing to do in studying peacetime organizational behavior is to examine less than effective leaders. It strikes me that poor leaders have a greater power to destroy than good leaders have the power to create. I understand that those of you who work for the federal government might find it a little awkward to start writing studies of ineffective military leaders. I have a strong suspicion that you might have a difficult time getting it past your advisory boards and the other people who look over your shoulders.

Colonel Borowski has also talked about the fruitfulness of examining the relationship between the leadership of the Air Force and that of corporate enterprise. There are two sets of phenomena at work. One is Air Force borrowing from corporate management practices. Certainly one can see signs of that in the pre-World War II period. It flourished during the Second World War and continued then in the post-World War II period. I want to remind all of our audience that it was the United States Army Air Forces that gave Robert McNamara his start.* One of the things that I think Harry Borowski does not adequately stress, however, is that there was already a well-established political purpose for creating the impression of organizational effectiveness and efficiency: the bottom line would always impress Congress. The Corps of Engineers had learned that lesson. The Navy bureaus at various times in their history have learned that lesson. Certainly Fred Ainsworth's Office of Pensions and Records in the War Department of the 1890s had learned that lesson.

A second set of phenomena is the continued collaboration between the Air Force and the aviation industry in the postwar period. That relationship deserves more study. Obviously histories of the creation of Systems Command and Logistics Command would require some attention to the impact of the collaborative and sometimes competitive relationship between the Air Force and its major suppliers. Certainly General Poe can speak to this far better than I. I would suggest that the pattern is not one of full collaboration but is one of major degrees of tension as well. By and large, I heartily endorse Colonel Borowski's call to do different kinds of military biographies and to meld the study of peacetime leaders with study of the growth and development of the institutions they serve.

Dr. Hone's paper on Rear Adm. William Moffett is a good example of the kind of biography that can be done of a peacetime military leader. I have no major criticisms of the paper. What I would like to do is stress matters of emphasis, not of correction. One thing that stood out in Moffett's career was his success as a builder of a Navy coalition supporting aviation. From the early 1920s until his death in the early 1930s, Moffett was one of a triad of

---

*Ed. note: Robert S. McNamara (1916–), Secretary of Defense 1961–68, was a lieutenant colonel and statistical control officer in the Army Air Forces during World War II.

successful Navy aviation organizational leaders. His power base was the Bureau of Aeronautics. At sea his major collaborator was Rear Adm. Joseph Mason Reeves, who in many ways was the organizational pioneer within the fleet.

Throughout the 1920s, with the exception of about a two-year period, Reeves had a major impact upon the development of naval aviation. Reeves, in fact, won the battle of large carrier versus small carrier. It is sometimes forgotten that the U.S. Navy with the *Saratoga* and the *Lexington* used up half the tonnage allotted to it under the Five-Power Treaty of the Washington Conference and that these two carriers cost in the neighborhood of $40 million each. This was a new high for warship construction; battleships in the same period cost only $27 million. There were certainly compelling reasons to find better ways to build carriers. Moffett, for example, began looking at smaller carriers and ways to multiply the number of decks available. Reeves had doubts about that policy, and I think he was primarily responsible for defining the optimal size of the carrier somewhere in the twenty-thousand-ton range rather than down toward fourteen thousand.

A third major participant in the naval aviation story was Adm. William S. Sims. Moffett did not have to be the Navy's Billy Mitchell, because the Navy already had one as President of the Naval War College. Sims spent his retirement as a very active publicist. One thing that is overlooked occasionally is that Sims' proteges staffed the important billets in naval aviation. So even though Sims himself was out of the picture, the second generation of "Young Turks" provided leadership.

Moffett played the role of adjudicator. Naval aviators as a group were split into two camps: the pioneers and the latecomers who had qualified in the program established in 1928 to send field grade officers to flight training. There was great tension between these two groups; yet Moffett successfully held them together and exploited both their capabilities. He was a Navy loyalist. Although he was a cultivator of congressmen, he also remained on good terms with the Navy's senior leaders. The Navy had a deserved reputation for quashing radicals. One needs only to study the relationship between David Dixon Porter and Benjamin Isherwood to realize what may happen when you make the boys on top mad.*

Moffett then combined traditional views of military leadership, bureaucratic deftness, and technical competence, though not as an aviator. Some people will call him new, some old. I think both of these are bothersome modifiers. What we have here is a clear case study of the fact that some

---

*Ed. note: After the Civil War, Adm. David Dixon Porter (1813–1891) used his influence to remove the Chief of the Bureau of Steam Engineering, Benjamin Franklin Isherwood (1822–1915). Porter favored putting sails on steamers.

AIR LEADERSHIP

officers are more fit by experience and perspective to be the organizational leaders in peace *and* war than other officers. Examples like Moffett can be found throughout the history of all America's armed forces.

Comment

Bryce Poe, II

I always find it difficult to say no to Al Hurley. When he grabbed me out there in the lobby a few minutes ago, he came close to straining the affection and respect I have for him. But he is a special fellow. Of all the myriad of visitors we had at my wing in Vietnam, Al Hurley was the only one that hung around and routinely flew combat missions. Further, he flew them in my old EC–47s, going at 90 knots to places where I was uncomfortable at 520 knots in my Phantom. That is really going to the primary source for historical information.

I was intrigued by the papers today. I think they began to open a door on some areas that are much too much neglected. Of course, I am biased because they cover changes I have seen—science and technology, politics, international affairs, and the rest—during my thirty-eight years in uniform. I think my generation had a unique chance to look at this. It is interesting when you consider that the first airplane I soloed was an open cockpit biplane Stearman and the last one I flew on active duty as a primary pilot was the Mach-three F–15 Eagle.

The world really changed during that period of time. I feel that the changes in what is required of leadership (not that more or less is required, but the changes) are as great perhaps as those of any other time in history. There is an enormous difference in the way the world goes. That is one of the things that is making it difficult for biographers. Science and technology's impact is not new. You can talk about Scipio Africanus' short sword of Spanish iron, or you can talk about the stirrup, but I think we must agree that with the lethality of today's weapons and the percentage of the national treasury at risk, you have a greater chance to be as outmoded as a battleship admiral or a horse cavalry general than ever before.

There are some philosophical changes that have been disturbing to me. There is a tendency to softsoap war and violence, the use of violence. We now have a Department of Defense, not a War Department. At Fort McNair we have the National Defense University. That is just a surface view of some of the things that have changed philosophically. I probably tried to use management techniques as much as any man who was on active duty—I had to in my jobs. Yet one of the problems of the manager has been trying to keep those management techniques from washing over into the conduct of violence.

It is one thing to get what you need and to work with allies under a bureaucratic system that is designed on the model of industry. It is another thing to try, as we have done in past years, to substitute these products of the Harvard Business School for lessons learned at an enormous cost in blood and treasure like the principles of war. We at first mongrelized them by adding the principle of defense—I still don't quite understand that. Then we proceeded to make changes in the way we looked at war itself. There is no substitute for business techniques in bringing men and equipment to the battlefield, but you have to meld carefully what happens when you get there.

The Russians were acting up one time in the 1970s when I was Vice Commander in Chief of U.S. Air Forces in Europe. I spent four days locked up in the readiness center without much to do. So I read every joint strategic operations plan in the nation's files. I was horrified to find—and I hate to admit this with my Navy friends here—that only the Navy in the Pacific had as a primary mission the destruction of enemy forces. Everybody else had some kind of esoteric mission for the application of violence. It is comforting to me (and I hope to you) that this has changed.

The centralization that comes with management still means a decentralization of action. Centralization under business techniques by nonbusiness people in the Department of Defense, most of the time not uniformed, has been a concern of great seriousness to me. First, it ignores two differences. One is difference in scale, and the other is difference in mission. Take the last first. Air Force units based in the United States, for example, will be in Europe within forty-eight hours of the beginning of a war. Comparable Army units will probably be there in thirty to sixty days, and the Navy will get some ships out of storage in maybe a year. That does not make one service better than the others. It makes them different. The application of management techniques has to take that into account.

The other difference is scale. I had a man give me a hard time one day: "You have got to follow the airlines in the management of engines." We learned a lot from the airlines, and his exact words were: "You have to find out how the big boys do it, or you are irresponsible." The problem was partly that we treated engines much differently than the airlines did; we were much harder on them. But the difference in the scale of our operations was just the opposite of what he had thought. He did not know until I told him that the largest airline in the free world is United and they have 1,300 engines; I was responsible for 44,000 jet engines. He wanted to add the Army's and Navy's 44,000 and manage the 88,000 out of one office in the Pentagon.

Another matter which we must pay attention to is communications. Thucydides once said that when the king is on the field, nothing is done without him. Now, through modern communications, the king may not only be on the most remote field, but he will have his whole bloody court with him, including National Security Council advisers, civilian appointees from the Office of the Secretary of Defense, think tank people, congressional staffers, and so forth. The media's role has been kicked to death; Sherman was just as upset about the media, even though there was no six o'clock news broadcast to the Military Division of the Mississippi. On the other hand, our relationship with allies is enormously different than in the past. There is not going to be any unilateral war, despite the fact that we still plan for unilateral war.

We need to think about how leadership should deal with these enormous changes. There is something which I call the "Fogbound Concept." If any of you are fans of "Li'l Abner," you will remember that Senator Fogbound won every election for many years by proclaiming, "You can't say I ever did anything wrong, because I never did anything." If we are not careful, we will build a system where there is no opportunity to fail. I got two Article 104s—for you young officers that's an Article 15 now—for doing things I thought were perfectly reasonable with aircraft. They chewed me out, they fined me, and they forgot it. Today that could well be the end of a career. General Gabriel* and his predecessor have tried to turn that around. Because if we get a commander with all the cardinal virtues, we probably will not get the kind of commander who is going to win the war.

Young people—many of them not so young now—have been brought up in an atmosphere where every failure is said to be a product of conspiracy, where the responsible people are said to be irresponsible. When was the last time you saw a senior officer—on television, in the press, or in a novel—who was not a buffoon or dishonest or cowardly? The respect of young people has to be earned. It can be done.

There is still a place for the plumed hat and the "follow me." That, I think, goes to what has been said here about flying. As an air leader, no matter how much work you have stacked up, you have got to fly more sorties than the other people in the wing, in wartime at any rate. In peacetime you probably cannot fly more sorties, but you can make every landing and every takeoff in every airplane you are in. You can be in the shops at night, you can be in the alert barn on weekends, and you can visit remote sites where people

---

*Ed. note: Gen. Charles A. Gabriel (1928–) replaced Gen. Lew Allen, Jr., (1925–) as Chief of Staff, USAF, on July 1, 1982.

AIR LEADERSHIP

are working on holidays. None of those things has changed, and they still apply to the quality of leadership.

As we pass through this management era, we have to understand that we cannot do the job without management techniques. But some of the baseline things we do for our job, which is the application of violence, have not changed very much. I would submit that we are pretty good at it. I doubt that there is an historical precedent for the iron discipline our aircrews showed both in Korea and in Southeast Asia—with all the weapons on the wings of their aircraft, taking losses because they were not allowed to attack enemy sanctuaries. There certainly was a professional military force out there with professional leadership.

Discussion

Dr. Alfred F. Hurley, Brig. Gen., USAF, Retired, chair
Lt. Col. Harry R. Borowski, USAF
Dr. Thomas C. Hone
Dr. Allan R. Millett
Gen. Bryce Poe, II, USAF, Retired

Question: Would you discuss the role of military education? General Arnold was a graduate of the Army Industrial College, now the Industrial College of the Armed Forces. The contribution of the Industrial College should be considered in relationship to the contribution of the National War College, formerly the Army War College.

Poe: I graduated from the National War College in residence and from the Industrial College through correspondence. Subsequently I made about equal use of the books I got from the two schools. But I sometimes felt that I needed to reinforce Industrial College graduates (who were the key to my work in Logistics Command) with people who had received war college training. I chose graduates of the war colleges as depot commanders, partly because they were best at talking to four-star generals. The two national schools are becoming more alike. The National War College has begun to teach more about the problems of acquisition, and the Industrial College is teaching more about how systems fit into the mission.

One aspect of military education has worried me for some time. I feel that we are a little better than we were, but I think we are still too narrow in the preparation of young officers. I would get young officers who were very narrowly trained in some engineering field. Then I would go to the Air Force Academy to talk to the history club, and they would say, "You know, I am taking more science and math here than I would at most state universities, but people are sneering at me because I am taking a soft history major." My reaction is that five years after graduation they will probably hire engineers to do the job for them. It doesn't mean we don't have engineers full time throughout their whole career in Systems Command. But when you look at the application of violence, which is really our job, you need to know more about how the world goes.

One of my difficulties with engineers, which was so serious that I took it to the Air Force Scientific Advisory Board—and they have done some things

AIR LEADERSHIP

about it—was that I would get people who had not had a course in English other than technical writing since high school. They were tremendous people and smarter than I would ever be on technical matters. But they could neither brief to get money nor write to solve a problem.

I have a quick anecdote about James Michener, the novelist. He was interviewed for a Navy direct commission in World War II with three other people—a buyer from Macy's, a lawyer, and another man. The Navy interviewer kept saying, "But can you do anything?" The lawyer said, "I sift evidence." The buyer said, "I determine trends." Michener said, "I can write." The fourth man was a diesel engineer, and the Navy signed him instantly. At the end of the war, the lawyer was one of Admiral King's key staff officers. The buyer had a similar success. Michener was on the staff of the Secretary of the Navy. And the other guy was still repairing diesel engines.

Hurley: Now you know why I was so pleased to have General Poe visit the Air Force Academy. He was very helpful to me in the curriculum discussions on what constituted the proper education for a future Air Force officer.

Question: Some years ago I was on what was then called the Army Industrial College faculty and ran across the most interesting piece of evidence about General Pershing in France during the First World War. Through a lack of industrial sensitivity, he would order production of aircraft just as if it could be turned on and off with the stroke of a pen. Of course, that caused total consternation back in the United States. Going forward in time, Eisenhower, while he never was a student at the Army Industrial College, did spend several months there on a special project and was sensitized to that problem. We didn't have any quick turn ons and turnoffs coming from him in World War II. It was the difference between night and day.

Hurley: Your comment reminds me of Colonel Shiner's new book on General Foulois.* I hope Colonel Shiner will someday look at Foulois' role in preparing those messages for Pershing's signature. I think, in reading that traffic myself, General Pershing was at a tremendous disadvantage with respect to the people who had been sent to him as experts. You will recall General Foulois' arrival in France with that very large delegation of people who intended to solve the air problems of the American Expeditionary Forces. General Pershing's name is on the cables, so he is responsible. But I think a serious investigation of General Foulois' development would highlight the need for the Industrial College.

Question: You quite appropriately talked about the influence of big business

---

*John F. Shiner, *Foulois and the U.S. Army Air Corps, 1931–1935* (Washington, D.C., 1983).

in shaping the military, but this is not a one-way street. There has been a long history in the United States of the military shaping business practices. Merritt Roe Smith's *Harper's Ferry Arsenal and the New Technology* provides some early examples.* I think what is really happening is that the two are coming together, not that one is taking over the other. David Noble, in *America by Design* and in his forthcoming work on numerically-controlled machine tools, finds the influence of the military forbidding. He establishes quite clearly that industry is responding to the military where it sees better procedures and techniques, just as the military is responding to business.†

Hurley: Indeed between business and the military there is a synergism which goes on whether one wants to acknowledge it or not. It does heighten the need for the kind of program that the Industrial College attempts to have.

Question: The American military has adopted business measures of merit which tend to focus on things that are as tangible as profits and losses. What might be efficient in peacetime is not necessarily going to be efficient in wartime. Martin van Creveld has commented about the German recognition of intangibles; Gabriel and Savage found that in Vietnam we were measuring things that had little relevance to success.‡ Is there a great danger in the military using business measures of merit?

Millett: I don't want to talk about Gabriel and Savage since I think *Crisis in Command* is a literary construct whose time has passed. But there is some validity in the question of the influence of performance evaluations on performance. It is well to remember that most of the people we have discussed spent their careers in services that promoted only by seniority and that neither the Navy nor the Army until the Second World War had anything like promotion for good performance. You could afford mistakes—Nimitz ran a ship aground as an ensign—because you could continue to be promoted as long as you weren't court-martialed and dismissed.§

There was a system within the Army, however, to identify people who were best suited for wartime command. In fact the personnel reports that were filed on officers in the Army had nothing to do with peacetime promotions but did have a great deal to do with rank in the volunteer army in

---

*Merritt Roe Smith, *Harper's Ferry Arsenal and the New Technology* (Ithaca, N.Y., 1977).

†David F. Noble, *America by Design: Science, Technology, and the Rise of Corporate Captitalism* (New York, 1977).

‡Martin van Creveld, *Fighting Power: German and U.S. Army Performance, 1939-1945* (Westport, Conn., 1982); Richard A. Gabriel and Paul L. Savage, *Crisis in Command: Mismanagement in the Army* (New York, 1978).

§Fleet Adm. Chester W. Nimitz (1885-1966) commanded the Pacific Fleet during World War II and became Chief of Naval Operations after that war. As an ensign in the Philippines before World War I, he had been court-martialed for running the destroyer *Decatur* aground.

war. There certainly was an inner elite that knew one another, and their personnel files indicated that they had been certified by a general officer or by a school for wartime command. In fact those lists were used both in 1898 and 1917. So there was an informal system of rewarding performance.

The problems we have today date back really to the Officer Personnel Act of 1947. "Deep selection" and "fast tracking" are more pronounced in some services than others and have been mixed blessings in terms of the cohesiveness of the officer corps, which is already riddled by overspecialization.* My guess is that we are moving back toward a middle position that will reflect a greater emphasis upon seniority and stability in assignments, just as business itself has recognized greater benefits in that pattern.

Poe: I think there are two subjects here. One is applying measures of merit to daily work. But if you are talking about the personnel angle, I must say that the toughest job I had in the last ten years of my career was deciding whom to move up. When I began in the service, one-half of one percent of Air Force officers were graduates of the academies, and about six percent had college degrees. By the time I had an advanced degree, only about six percent had an advanced degree; so I was ahead of that wave. I sometimes wonder if I could even get in one of the academies today or make corporal.

The competition is enormously keen, and what you wind up with is looking at say five thousand people for five hundred promotions, school slots, whatever it is. You rate the people from 0 to 10. You have three or four that pop out on top because of something exceptional and a few that drop off the bottom because you wonder why we haven't gotten rid of them. Out of that five thousand you have probably two thousand who could take that additional rank or school and do tremendously. When you look at the ratings you have given them (let's say they go from 7.5 to 9), the bottom of the top five hundred is 8.5, but fifteen hundred below is 8.3. You begin to look for tie breakers.

In the past few years, we have tried to ensure more logical career development. The position of wing commander, for example, is a key to stars in the Air Force. So we are not inclined to let a man be a wing commander unless he has been a base commander, or a deputy chief of staff for maintenance, or something comparable. Before, a lot of us went up in rank by flying airplanes. Then people wondered why things fell to pieces when we had to solve problems involving people, or money, or the rest of it.

---

*The Officer Personnel Act of 1947 favored promotion by selection over promotion by seniority. The newly independent Air Force broke away from the seniority system immediately through a one-time selection of lieutenants and captains for promotion to majors, lieutenant colonels, and colonels.

PATTERNS

We have had to get tougher. When I put on my first star, there were about 450 Air Force generals. Now there are maybe 340. You can't reward the horse holder any more, and you can't pat some technician on the back to make all the rest of the technicians in his area feel good about it. When you pin down a handful of people for stars, you have to apply very rigorous techniques. Most businessmen who come in and help us in the Air Force as Secretary, Under Secretary, and so forth are very complimentary of our promotion system in the higher grades. They say they have nothing to compare with it in business. After two and a half years with business I am inclined to agree, because there are very strange people at high levels.

Question: General Poe's comments on the application of business techniques to the conduct of violence struck a very responsive cord in my heart because of my experience as a flight-line maintenance officer in Vietnam. I shall carry to my grave the memory of the weeks we spent preparing a display for Gen. Joseph Nazzaro when he was Commander in Chief of the Pacific Air Forces.* We lined up F–100 aircraft with representative loads on board. The wing vice commander was in charge of this project. He would come down to the flight line and spend five minutes rearranging aircraft symbols on a little card, and then we would spend days rearranging the aircraft themselves. The upshot of this was that General Nazzaro's staff car went racing down the road for thirty seconds. He never saw the guys in the starched fatigues, or the aircraft loads, or anything else. Would you comment on how we make the transition from the business techniques that we need in peacetime to the leadership techniques that we need in times that are vital?

Poe: We need to make sure that a man who gets in a command position has been on the flight line. He should know that for every four bombs loaded, only one is dropped if the required bomb loads keep changing. Then he doesn't ask for displays. Nor does he keep changing the bomb loads.

I could not have done my job without business techniques, and business management knows that these are not simple problems. A commander's experience is critical. When I arrived in Europe to take an F–4 wing, we required every pilot to know forty-two loads (combinations of bombs, napalm, and missiles). Nobody could do that. Then for the first time, we got people in charge who had been on the flight line, and we got it down to seven basic loads.

We must be very careful of the person who has been catapulted to high command on the "Fogbound" theory. He has avoided risk, he has avoided command, he has avoided standing up and briefing key people, and all of a sudden, he finds himself up there where all these omissions come home to

---

*Gen. Joseph J. Nazzaro (1913–) was Commander in Chief, Pacific Air Forces, 1968–71.

AIR LEADERSHIP

roost. He will usually get fired in about a year, but during that year, you will have exercises like the one you have described.

Question: One of the strongest actions that a military leader can take in peacetime is resignation. At least it does a lot for the morale of junior officers. Is this seen as an effective action, and if so, why have we not seen more examples?

Poe: Somebody once asked me what was my biggest problem as a commander, and I said patience. It is not a virtue normally found in the professional soldier, and it is one that you must develop. Let me give you a personal example. After my spending a couple of years as a four-star general at the Air Force Logistics Command, two upsetting things happened in one week. First, the President submitted to the Congress a budget request for only fifteen percent of the Air Force's validated requirement for spare parts in the first thirty days of a war. Then he invented honorable discharges for those who had got out to avoid service in Southeast Asia. I am the fourth generation of my family to wear the uniform. I looked at my great-grandfather's discharge on the wall of my study, and I said, "I have got to go."

Fortunately the next day that wisest of airmen, Gen. Ira Eaker, came through. He put his finger in a glass of water, pulled it out again and said, "Bryce, for a four-star general to quit today, it will make just about that much difference. You are better prepared for this job than anybody we have had in it before. If you stay on and fight it, maybe you can do something about it." A year later, even before the change in administration, we had, by taking it head-on publicly, tripled the amount of money for spares. It was still desperately low, but we had done some good.

I don't think people are afraid to quit. My God, my service as a three-star and four-star general was done at exactly the same pay as 1,500 other people in my 89,000–man command, right down through senior colonels. I don't know what keeps you there except the desire to do the job. I think most people would quit if they thought quitting would help. Maybe more of us should have, but that was the thinking in an instance I know about.

Borowski: In the fall of 1981 at a Naval Academy symposium, the very same issue came up. A gentleman at the back of the room raised his hand and asked to address the group. It was Adm. Arleigh Burke.* He came forward and told a story that is very similar to what General Poe has just related. The upshot was that the admiral had once been so dismayed that he had felt resignation was really in order. Then he went home and discussed it with his wife. They concluded that his resignation might make a story in the

---

*Adm. Arleigh A. Burke (1901–) was Chief of Naval Operations, 1955–61.

Washington Post and might cause a flap for two or three days. But the President would appoint a replacement whose thinking was more in line with the President's. So it didn't take Burke very long to decide to stay in and fight for his position. Obviously that gave him the appearance of being supportive of the President's posture or not being strong enough to stand up against it.

There are civilian examples of resignation. Stuart Symington resigned as Secretary of the Air Force in the spring of 1950 ostensibly over President Truman's reluctance to submit a budget which was in consonance with our military responsibilities. We don't know what impact Symington's resignation would have had if the subsequent onset of the Korean War had not boosted appropriations anyway. But my assessment is that Symington's resignation had no impact on Truman at all.

The issue of resignation is frequently raised by cadets at the Air Force Academy. It is a disservice to our general officers to suggest that not taking such stands stems from a lack of integrity.

Poe: You must never forget that in the military you have two responsibilities that you don't have other places. One of them is that if you don't agree with a policy, you have to offer alternatives. The other one is that once you are overruled, unless you quit, you have to carry out that policy to the best of your ability. That's unique to this profession. It probably shouldn't be, but it is.

Suggestions for Further Reading

Arnold, Gen Henry H. *Global Mission*. New York: Harper, 1949.
Blumenson, Martin, and James L. Stokesbury. *Masters of the Art of Command*. Boston: Houghton Mifflin, 1975.
Boyle, Andrew. *Trenchard*. London: Collins, 1962.
Bradley, Gen Mark E. "The P–51 Over Berlin." *Aerospace Historian*, 21 (Sep 74).
Brown, Richard C. *Social Attitudes of American Generals, 1898–1940*. New York: Arno, 1970. (PhD dissertation, Wisconsin, 1951).
Buck, James H., and Lawrence J. Korb. *Military Leadership*. Beverly Hills, Calif.: Sage, 1981.
Burns, James MacGregor. *Leadership*. New York: Harper and Row, 1978.
Carver, Field Marshal Sir Michael. *The War Lords: Military Commanders of the Twentieth Century*. Boston: Little, Brown, 1976.
Chennault, Maj Gen Claire L. *Way of a Fighter*. New York: Putnam, 1949.
Coffey, Thomas M. *Hap: The Story of the U.S. Air Force and the Man Who Built It*. New York: Viking, 1982.
———. *Iron Eagle: The Turbulent Life of General Curtis LeMay*. New York: Crown, 1986.
Collier, Basil. *Leader of the Few: The Authorized Biography of Air Chief Marshal, the Lord Dowding of Bentley Priory*. London: Jarrolds, 1957.
Copp, DeWitt S. *A Few Great Captains: The Men and Events that Shaped the Development of U.S. Air Power*. Garden City, N.Y.: Doubleday, 1980.
———. *Forged in Fire: Strategy and Decisions in the Air War over Europe, 1940–45*. Garden City, N.Y.: Doubleday, 1982.
Davis, Richard G. "The Bomber Baron: Carl Spaatz and the Army Air Forces in Europe, 1942–45." (PhD dissertation, George Washington, 1986).
Flanagan, Lt Gen Edward M., Jr. *Before the Battle: A Commonsense Guide to Leadership and Management*. Novato, Calif.: Presidio, 1985.
Fuller, Maj Gen J. F. C. *Generalship: Its Diseases and Their Cure*. Harrisburg, Pa.: Military Services Publishing Company, 1936.
Galland, Gen Adolf. *The First and the Last: The Rise and Fall of the German Fighter Forces, 1938–1945*. Translated by Mervyn Savill. New York: Holt, 1954.
Geffen, William, ed. *Command and Commanders in Modern Warfare:*

Proceedings of the Second Military History Symposium. Colorado Springs: U.S. Air Force Academy, 1969.

Glines, Carroll V. *Jimmy Doolittle: Master of the Calculated Risk.* New York: Van Nostrand Reinhold, 1980.

Hackett, Gen Sir John. *The Profession of Arms.* New York: Macmillan, 1983.

Hansell, Maj Gen Haywood S., Jr. *The Air Plan that Defeated Hitler.* Atlanta: Higgins-McArthur, 1972.

Harris, Marshal of the RAF Sir Arthur. *Bomber Offensive.* London: Collins, 1947.

Hiroyoki Agawa. *The Reluctant Admiral: Yamamoto and the Imperial Navy.* Tokyo: Kodansha International, 1979.

Horsfield, John. *The Art of Leadership in War: The Royal Navy from the Age of Nelson to the End of World War II.* Westport, Conn.: Greenwood, 1980.

Huntington, Samuel P. *The Soldier and the State: The Theory and Politics of Civil-Military Relations.* Cambridge, Mass.: Harvard, 1957.

Hurley, Alfred F., and Robert C. Erhart. *Air Power and Warfare: Proceedings of the Eighth Military History Symposium, U.S. Air Force Academy.* Washington: Office of Air Force History, 1979.

Hurley, Alfred F. *Billy Mitchell: Crusader for Air Power.* Revised edition. Bloomington: Indiana University, 1975.

Janowitz, Morris. *The Professional Soldier: A Social and Political Portrait.* New York: Free Press, 1960.

Kenney, Gen George C. *General Kenney Reports: A Personal History of the Pacific War.* New York: Duell, Sloan and Pearce, 1949.

Kohn, Richard H., and Joseph P. Harahan, eds. *Air Superiority in World War II and Korea: An Interview with Gen James Ferguson, Gen Robert M. Lee, Gen William Momyer, and Lt Gen Elwood R. Quesada.* Washington: Office of Air Force History, 1983.

LeMay, Gen Curtis E., with MacKinlay Kantor. *Mission with LeMay.* Garden City, N.Y.: Doubleday, 1965.

Love, Robert William, Jr., ed. *The Chiefs of Naval Operations.* Annapolis: Naval Institute Press, 1980.

McGovern, James R. *Black Eagle: General Daniel "Chappie" James, Jr.* University, Ala.: University of Alabama, 1985.

Macksey, Kenneth John. *Kesselring: The Making of the Luftwaffe.* New York: David McKay, 1978.

Mahurin, Walker M. *Honest John.* New York: Putnam, 1962.

Meilinger, Phillip S. "Hoyt S. Vandenberg: The Life of a General." PhD dissertation, Michigan, 1985.

Momyer, Gen William W. *Airpower in Three Wars.* Washington: U.S. Air Force, 1978.

Newman, Maj Gen Aubrey S. *Follow Me: The Human Element in Leadership.* Novato, Calif.: Presidio, 1981.

Overy, R. J. *Goering: The "Iron Man".* London: Routledge and Kegan Paul, 1984.

Parrish, Brig Gen Noel Francis. *Behind the Sheltering Bomb: Military Indecision from Alamagordo to Korea.* New York: Arno, 1979. (PhD dissertation, Rice, 1968.)

Parton, James. *"Air Force Spoken Here" General Ira Eaker and the Command of the Air.* Washington, DC: Adler and Adler, 1986.

Power, Gen Thomas S., with Albert A. Arnhym. *Design for Survival.* New York: Coward-McCann, 1965.

Puryear, Edgar F., Jr. *George S. Brown: General, U.S. Air Force.* Novato, Calif: Presidio, 1983.

———. *Stars in Flight: A Study in Air Force Character and Leadership.* Novato, Calif.: Presidio, 1981.

Radford, Adm Arthur W. *From Pearl Harbor to Vietnam.* Edited by Stephen Jurika, Jr. Stanford: Hoover Institution, 1980.

Reynolds, Clark G. *Famous American Admirals.* New York: Van Nostrand Reinhold, 1978.

———. *The Fast Carriers: The Forging of an Air Navy.* New York: McGraw-Hill, 1968.

Reynolds, Jon. "Education and Training for High Command: General Hoyt S. Vandenberg's Early Career." (PhD dissertation, Duke, 1980).

Richards, Denis. *Portal of Hungerford.* London: Heinemann, 1977.

Risner, Brig Gen Robinson. *The Passing of the Night: My Seven Years as a Prisoner of the North Vietnamese.* New York: Random House, 1974.

Roskill, Stephen W. *The Art of Leadership.* London: Collins, 1964.

Saward, Dudley. *Bomber Harris: The Story of Marshal of the Royal Air Force Sir Arthur Harris.* New York: Doubleday, 1985.

Scott, Brig Gen Robert Lee, Jr. *Flying Tiger: Chennault of China.* Garden City, N.Y.: Doubleday, 1959.

———. *God is My Co-Pilot.* New York: Scribner, 1943.

Shiner, John F. *Foulois and the U.S. Army Air Corps, 1931–1935.* Washington: Office of Air Force History, 1983.

Slessor, Marshal of the RAF Sir John. *The Central Blue.* London: Cassell, 1956.

Stockdale, Vice Adm James B. *A Vietnam Experience: Ten Years of Reflection.* Stanford: Hoover Institution, 1984.

Stockdale, Vice Adm James B. and Sybil. *In Love and War.* New York: Harper and Row, 1984.

Stogdill, Ralph Melvin. *Stogdill's Handbook of Leadership: A Survey of Theory and Research.* Revised ed. New York, N.Y.: Free Press, 1981.

Taylor, Robert L., and William E. Rosenbach, eds. *Military Leadership: In Pursuit of Excellence.* Boulder, Colo.: Westview, 1984.

Taylor, Theodore. *The Magnificent Mitscher.* New York: Norton, 1954.

Tedder, Marshal of the RAF Lord. *With Prejudice.* London: Cassell, 1966.

Terraine, John. *A Time for Courage: The Royal Air Force in the European War, 1939–1945.* New York: Macmillan, 1985.

Thomas, Lowell and Edward Jablonski. *Doolittle: A Biography.* Garden City, N.Y.: Doubleday, 1976.

Tunner, Lt Gen William H. *Over the Hump.* New York: Duell, Sloan and Pearce, 1964. (Reprinted by the Office of Air Force History, 1985).

Van Creveld, Martin L. *Command in War.* Cambridge, Mass.: Harvard, 1985.

Wavell, Gen Sir Archibald. *Generals and Generalship.* New York: Macmillan, 1941.

Williams, T. Harry. "The Macs and the Ikes: America's Two Military Traditions." *American Mercury* LXXV (Oct 52), 32–39.

Wolk, Herman S. *Planning and Organizing the Postwar Air Force, 1943–1947.* Washington: Office of Air Force History, 1984.

Participants

LT. COL. HARRY R. BOROWSKI is Deputy Head of the History Department at the U.S. Air Force Academy. He holds a PhD from the University of California, Santa Barbara. His publications include *A Hollow Threat: Strategic Air Power and Containment before Korea* (Westport, Conn., 1982).

GEN. MARK E. BRADLEY, JR., was Commander, Air Force Logistics Command, from 1962 until his retirement in 1965. After graduating from West Point in 1930, he became a test pilot and project officer at Wright Field, Ohio. During World War II (when he served in both the European and Pacific theaters), he helped to extend the range of the F–51 Mustang escort fighter. After the war, he contributed to the development of air-to-air refueling.

DR. WILLIAM S. DUDLEY is Head of the Naval Historical Center's Research Branch and former Chairman of the Military Classics Seminar. He took his PhD from Columbia University and taught at Southern Methodist University. His most recent publication is the first volume of *The Naval War of 1812: A Documentary History* (Washington, 1985).

DR. ALFRED GOLDBERG is Historian, Office of the Secretary of Defense. During World War II, he served as an Army Air Forces historical officer in England. He contributed to four of the seven volumes of *The Army Air Forces in World War II* (Chicago, 1948–58), and he edited *A History of the United States Air Force, 1907–1957* (Princeton, 1957). In 1958 he founded the Military Classics Seminar. His essay "Spaatz" appeared in Field Marshal Sir Michael Carver, editor, *The War Lords* (Boston, 1976).

BRIG. GEN. BRIAN S. GUNDERSON is President of the Air Force Historical Foundation. He was Chief of the Office of Air Force History before retiring in 1974. His article "Eighth Air Force Newsboys—Cheddington Revisited" (*Aerospace Historian*, Dec 1984) recounts his World War II service as a navigator in B–17s dropping propaganda leaflets.

DR. IRVING B. HOLLEY, JR., teaches history at Duke University. After serving in the Army Air Forces in World War II, he remained in the Reserve and rose to the rank of major general before retiring in 1981. A Yale PhD, he is the author of *Ideas and Weapons: Exploitation of the Aerial Weapon by the United States During World War I* (New Haven, 1953), *Buying Aircraft: Air Materiel Procurement for the Army Air Forces* (Washington, 1964), and

AIR LEADERSHIP

General John M. Palmer, Citizen Soldiers, and the Army of a Democracy (Westport, Conn., 1982).

DR. THOMAS C. HONE teaches at the Naval War College. Since 1973 when he received his PhD in political science from the University of Wisconsin, he has published many articles on the interwar Navy.

DR. ALFRED F. HURLEY is Chancellor of North Texas State University. He was Head of the History Department at the U.S. Air Force Academy for more than a decade before his retirement as a brigadier general in 1980. A Princeton PhD, he is the author of *Billy Mitchell: Crusader for Air Power* (New York, 1964).

GEN. CURTIS E. LEMAY was Chief of Staff of the Air Force before retiring in 1965. Already famous for his air leadership in both theaters of World War II, he took charge of Strategic Air Command in 1948. In the next decade he built it into the most formidable military force in the world. With MacKinlay Kantor, he published his memoirs, *Mission with LeMay* (Garden City, N.Y., 1965).

DR. DAVID R. METS is writing a biography of General Spaatz for the Air Force Historical Foundation. Dr. Mets retired from the Air Force as a lieutenant colonel in 1979. He was the editor of *Air University Review* and has taught history at both the U.S. Air Force Academy and West Point.

DR. ALAN R. MILLETT is director of the Program in International Security and Military Affairs, Mershon Center, Ohio State University. A colonel in the Marine Corps Reserve, he is the author of *Semper Fidelis: A History of the U.S. Marine Corps* (New York, 1980) and co-author with Peter Maslowski of *For the Common Defense: A Military History of the United States of America* (New York, 1984).

GEN. BRYCE POE, II, was Commander of Air Force Logistics Command from 1978 until his retirement in 1981. After graduating from West Point in 1946, he became one of the first jet pilots. At the beginning of the Korean War, he flew the Air Force's initial jet combat reconnaissance sortie. He later participated extensively in the development and employment of the early intercontinental ballistic missiles. During the war in Southeast Asia, he returned to tactical reconnaissance and commanded a wing in South Vietnam.

AIR COMMODORE HENRY A. PROBERT is Head of the Air Historical Branch, Ministry of Defence, United Kingdom. He joined the Royal Air Force in 1948 after graduating from Cambridge with honors. His service took him to Northern Ireland, Germany, and Singapore. He was Director of RAF Education before retiring in 1978.

Index

Adams, Porter: 96
Ainsworth, Maj. Gen. Fred C.: 132
Air Force Academy: 139, 140
Air Force Scientific Advisory Board: 139
Air Forces
    Eighth: 25, 27, 28, 42
    Fifteenth: 28
    Twelfth: 26
Air Service Tactical School: 22
Akron: 108
Anderson, Fred: 66
Archibald, James F.J.: 110
Army Industrial College: 140
Arnold, Gen. Henry H. "Hap": 5, 9, 20, 42, 44, 48, 52, 65, 68, 81, 122, 131, 139
Atomic bomb: 42

Badoglio, Marshal Pietro: 16
Baldwin, Stanley: 64
Battle of Britain: 67, 77, 78
Benson, Adm. W.S.: 86, 90
Borowski, Lt. Col. Harry R.: 131, 132
Biddle, Capt. Charles J.: 4
Bingham, Hiram: 52, 53
Boyle, Andrew: 60
Bradley, Gen. Omar N.: 28, 123
Braisted, W.R.: 85, 104
Bureau of Aeronautics (BUAER): 92, 93, 100, 104, 106, 107, 111

Bureau of Navigation (BUNAV): 97
Burke, Adm. Arleigh: 144, 145
Burns, Robert: 17

Castle, Fred: 45
Chandler, Alfred D.: 121, 122, 123
Churchill, Winston: 16, 60, 68, 69, 76
Ciano, Count Galeazzo: 16
Cohu, LaMont: 125
Combined Bomber Offensive: 28, 31
Cook, Orval: 45
Coolidge, President Calvin: 99, 106
Coontz, Adm. R.E.: 97, 109
Copp, Pete: 59, 61, 62, 63, 64, 65, 66, 67, 68, 69
Craigie, Laurence C.: 126
Creveld, Martin van: 141
Cromwell, Oliver: 19

Daniels, Josephus: 85
Denby, Edwin: 92, 97
D'Olier, Franklin: 10
Doolittle, Maj. Gen. James H.: 8, 66
Dowding, Air Chief Marshal Lord: 17, 63, 77
Drop tank issue: 31, 32–33, 41, 54

AIR LEADERSHIP

Eaker, Gen. Ira C.: 5, 26, 52, 58, 66, 125, 126, 144
Eberle Board: 97
Eberle, Adm. E.W.: 97, 109
Eisenhower, Gen. Dwight D.: 6, 7, 8, 9, 20, 26, 27, 52, 55, 120

Fiske, Rear Adm. B.A.: 94
Forrestal, James V.: 43
Foulois, Maj. Gen. Benjamin: 46, 63, 140
Frankland, Noble: 60

Gabriel, Gen. Charles A.: 137
Gabriel, Richard A.: 141
Gherardi, Capt. Walter Rockwell: 110
Gilbert, Martin: 76
Giles, Lt. Gen. Barney: 9
Goldberg, Alfred: 10, 81
Great Lakes Aeronautical Society: 84

Harding, President Warren G.: 92
Harris, Air Marshal Sir Arthur "Bomber": 19–20, 60, 66, 69, 73
Haugen, Orin: 45
Henderson, Gen. Sir David: 61
Hicks, Rep. Frederick C.: 90
Hildy, Ralph and Muriel: 121
Hitler, Adolf: 54, 69
Holley, Maj. Gen. I.B.: 53, 54, 110
Holmes, Oliver Wendell, Jr.: 19
Hoover, President Herbert: 108
Hughes, Adm. C.F.: 104, 106, 109, 110

Hurley, Brig. Gen. Alfred F.: 81–82, 135
Hyde, H. Montgomery: 60

Industrial College of the Armed Forces: 139
Ingalls, D.S.: 103
Inskip, Sir Thomas: 67
Isherwood, Benjamin: 133

Johnson, Air Vice Marshal Johnnie: 77
Johnson Board: 99
Johnson, Capt. A.W.: 97
Joint Army and Navy Board of Aeronautics: 96
Jones, R.V.: 60

Kantor, MacKinlay: 39–40
Kassel strike: 27
Kennedy, Joseph P.: 22
Kenney, Gen. George C.: 123
Kiel strike: 27
Kilner, Mike: 53
King, Adm. Ernest J.: 62

Lampert Committee: 97, 99, 101
Land, Capt. Emory S.: 106, 108
Laning, Harris: 109
Lawrence, Col. T.E.: 17
Leigh, Rear Adm.: 104, 105, 110
Leigh–Mallory, Air Chief Sir Trafford: 8
Leighton, Lt. Col. B.G.: 93, 103
LeMay, Gen. Curtis E.: 125, 131
Lexington: 108, 133
Lloyd, Sir Hugh: 42

INDEX

Lord, Clifford: 91
Lovett, Robert A.: 42, 123, 124

MacArthur, Gen. Douglas: 20, 108
Marshall, Gen. George C.: 7, 9, 10, 49, 110, 119, 122
Marshall, Rear Adm. A.W.: 110
Mayo, Adm. H.T.: 87, 89
McMullen, Maj. Gen. Clements: 123
McNamara, Robert: 132
Melhorn, Charles: 90, 96
Mets, Lt. Col. David R.: 41, 43, 44
Michener, James: 140
Mitchell, Brig. Gen. William "Billy": 5, 11, 21, 31, 81, 84, 89, 90, 91, 94, 96, 97, 98, 103, 133
Moffett, Rear Adm. William A.: 80, 83–113, 132–33, 134
Montgomery, Field Marshal Bernard L.: 123
Moorer, Adm. Thomas H.: 82
Morrow Board: 62, 99, 101, 104
Morrow, Dwight: 99
Mustin, Cdr. H.C.: 93, 94, 103

Napoleon: 3, 4
National Advisory Committee for Aeronautics (NACA): 92, 96
National War College: 139
Nazzaro, Gen. Joseph J.: 143
Newall, Cyril: 63
Nimitz, Adm. Chester W.: 122
Noble, David: 141
Normandy: 8
Norstad, Maj. Gen. Lauris: 125

Nye, Senator Gerald: 120

Operation Overlord: 29
Owen, Russell: 110

Patrick, Gen. Mason: 50
Patton, Gen. George S., Jr.: 6, 7, 44
Pearl Harbor attack: 23, 65
Pershing, Gen. John J.: 15, 122, 140
Phoney War: 22
Poe, Gen. Bryce: 132, 140, 144
Pogue, Forrest: 49, 119
Poincare, Jules: 17
Portal, Sir Charles: 60, 68
Porter, Adm. David Dixon: 133
Power, Brig. Gen. Tommy: 42
Powers, Brig. Gen. Edward M.: 126
Pratt, Adm. W.V.: 108
Pride, Adm. A.M.: 104
Probert, Air Commodore Henry A.: 73, 74, 76–77, 78, 81

Radford, Adm. Arthur: 10
Ranger: 108
Reeves, Capt. Joseph Mason: 101, 104, 133
Richards, Denis: 60
Rickenbacker, Edward V.: 81
Rickover, Rear Adm. H.G.: 112
Rockefeller, John D.: 121, 124
Rodman, Rear Adm. Hugh: 87
Roosevelt, President Franklin D.: 10
Roskill, Stephen: 109

Sapolsky, Harvey: 113

AIR LEADERSHIP

Saratoga: 108, 133
Savage, Paul L.: 141
Saward, Dudley: 73, 74
Schweinfurt raids: 27
Shenandoah: 99, 103
Shiner, Col. John F.: 140
Sims, Adm. W.S.: 88, 94, 101, 109, 133
Sinclair, Archibald: 66
Slessor, Sir John: 59, 60, 61, 65, 67
Sloan, Alfred P., Jr.: 123
Smith, Merritt Roe: 141
Smith, Lt. Gen. Walter Bedell: 123
Smuts, Lt. Gen. J.C.: 60–61, 64
Spaatz, Gen. Carl A.: 2, 3–11, 15–34, 41, 42, 43, 44, 45, 46, 48, 49, 50–51, 52, 53, 54, 65, 67, 68, 76, 81, 124, 126
Spaatz, Ruth: 5
Stalin, Josef: 68
Street, Maj. Gen. St. Clair: 124
Swinton, Lord (Philip Cunliffe-Lister): 63
Symington, Stuart: 49, 126

Taylor, Rear Adm. D.W.: 91
Taylor, Rear Adm. Montgomery M.: 99
Tedder, Air Chief Marshal Sir Arthur: 8
Terraine, John: 68
Tinker, Clarence: 49
Towers, Cmdr. J.H.: 88, 93, 94

Trenchard, Lord: 60, 61, 63, 66
Truman, President Harry S: 42
Twining, Gen. Nathan F.: 42, 81, 126

United States Strategic Air Forces in Europe (USSTAF): 28, 29, 30
United States Strategic Bombing Survey: 30
ULTRA: 8

Vandenberg, Gen. Hoyt S.: 31, 32
Vinson, Carl: 109

Webster, Sir Charles: 60
Westmoreland, Gen. William C.: 122
Westover, Brig. Gen. Oscar: 46

Weyland, Gen. Otto P.: 126
Whiting, Cmdr. Kenneth: 88, 93
Wilbur, Curtis D.: 97, 106, 107, 108
Wood, Robert E.: 45, 123
Wrigley, William: 84, 85, 103, 106, 107

Yarnell, Capt. Harry E.: 101

Zuckerman, Solly: 74